Alfred's Basic Piano Library

T0024358

THE COMPLETE BOOK OF
SCALES, CHORDS, ARPEGGIOS & CADENCES

Includes all the Major, Minor (Natural, Harmonic, Melodic) & Chromatic Scales — plus additional instructions on music fundamentals

WILLARD A. PALMER • MORTON MANUS • AMANDA VICK LETHCO

How This Book Is Organized

Part 1
An explanation that leads to the understanding of the fundamentals of major and minor scales, chords, arpeggios and cadences is discussed in some detail. Also included is a clear explanation of scale degrees and a two-page guide to fingering the scales and arpeggios. *Pages 4–17*

Part 2
The Major Scales: The key of C plus the sharp keys in key signature sequence. *Pages 18–33*

Part 3
The Major Scales: The flat keys in key signature sequence. *Pages 34–47*

Part 4
The Minor Scales: The key of A minor plus the sharp keys in key signature sequence. *Pages 48–63*

Part 5
The Minor Scales: The flat keys in key signature sequence. *Pages 64–77*

Part 6
The Chromatic Scales: *Pages 78–79*

Part 7
Enrichment Options: These added options are designed to further develop musicianship. They suggest a number of additional ways the scales and chords in parts 2–5 may be played. Some of the options should be practiced in every key being studied. *Pages 80–89*

Cover design: Martha Widmann/Ted Engelbart
Book production: Bruce Goldes

Foreword

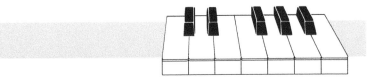

"I don't like to practice, never have. But when I do get started at the piano, for the first 10 minutes I play scales, slowly. I've done this all my life. Listen to the sounds you make. The sound of each tone will generate a response in you. It will give you energy."
Van Cliburn

"Do you ask me how good a player you may become? Then tell me how much you practice the scales."
Carl Czerny

"I consider the practice of scales important not only for the fingers, but also for the discipline of the ear with regard to the feeling of tonality (key), understanding of intervals, and the comprehension of the total compass of the piano."
Josef Hofmann

"Give special study to passing the thumb under the hand and passing the hand over the thumb. This makes the practice of scales and arpeggios indispensable."
Jan Paderewski

"Scales should never be dry. If you are not interested in them, work with them until you do become interested in them."
Artur Rubinstein

"I believe this matter of insisting upon a thorough technical knowledge, particularly scale playing, is a very vital one. The mere ability to play a few pieces does not constitute musical proficiency."
Sergei Rachmaninoff

"You must diligently practice all scales."
Robert Schumann

The importance of scales and arpeggios, particularly with regard to the pianist's ability to perform, cannot be over-estimated. To trace the development of the major and minor scales through the history of music would require many pages, but we do know that these scales had their origins in the system of modes that was developed in ancient Greek music and music of the Church.

In ancient Greece, certain musical tribes used a lyre, a four-stringed harp called the *tetrachordon* (*tetra* meaning four). The four tones encompassed by this instrument constituted a perfect 4th, and were called a tetrachord. This was the building block that was to become the basis for our modern scales.

On the keyboard, a tetrachord consists of a whole step, a whole step and a half step. If we play a tetrachord beginning on C, we have the notes C, D, E and F. If we begin a second tetrachord on G, we have the notes G, A, B and C. The last C of this tetrachord is exactly one octave higher than the low C of the first tetrachord. These two tetrachords, played in succession, make an eight-note scale in the Ionian mode, which we now know as a major scale. If we use the same tones beginning on the 6th note of the combined two tetrachords, we get the notes A, B, C, D, E, F, G and A. These notes constitute the Aeolian mode, which is also known as our natural minor scale.

The Greek philosopher Pythagorus (around 500 BC) is credited with the discovery of the numerical ratios corresponding to the principal intervals of the musical scale. With an instrument known as a *monochord*, consisting of one string stretched over a long sounding-board, Pythagorus found that by dividing the string into 2 equal parts, one part, when vibrated, would give a tone exactly one octave above the natural tone of the whole string. By sounding 2/3 of the length of the string, the interval of a 5th above the natural tone would be produced. By sounding 3/4 of the length of the string, the interval of a 4th would be produced. In similar manner, the ratios of all the notes of the scale were discovered.

With the ongoing evolution of stringed and keyboard instruments, our modern major and minor scales were developed, and the various temperaments associated with all of the ancient and modern tunings were ultimately derived.

Contents

4

Part 1 — Tetrachords

The word *tetra* means four. A TETRACHORD is a series of FOUR NOTES having a pattern of

WHOLE STEP, WHOLE STEP, HALF STEP

A **HALF STEP** is the distance from any key to the very next key up or down, black or white, with **NO KEY BETWEEN**.

A **WHOLE STEP** is equal to 2 HALF STEPS with **ONE KEY BETWEEN**.

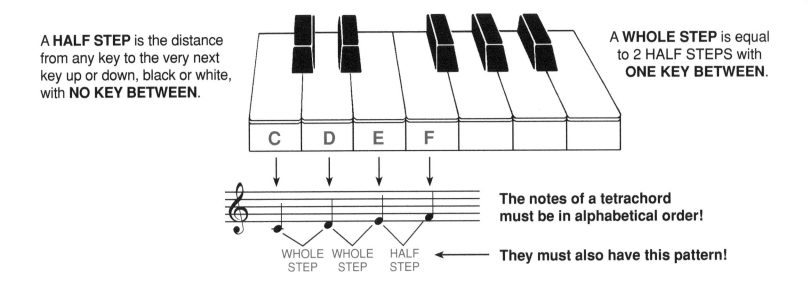

The notes of a tetrachord must be in alphabetical order!

They must also have this pattern!

C Tetrachord

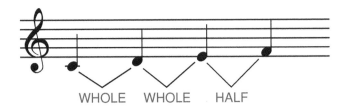

G Tetrachord

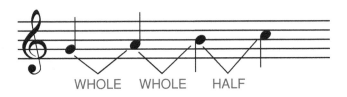

D Tetrachord

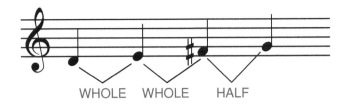

A Tetrachord

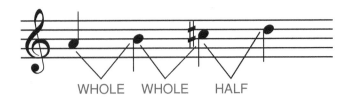

E Tetrachord

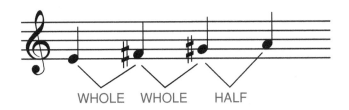

B Tetrachord

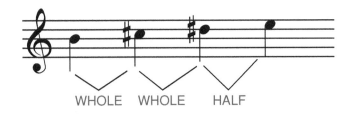

Building Major Scales

The MAJOR SCALE is made of **TWO TETRACHORDS** *joined* by a **WHOLE STEP**.

The C Major Scale

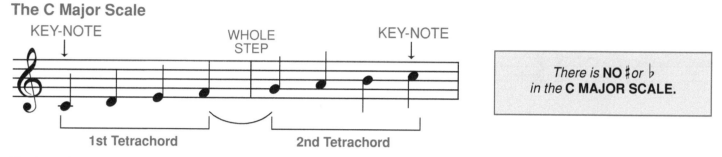

> There is **NO** ♯ *or* ♭ *in the* **C MAJOR SCALE.**

Each scale begins and ends on the note of the same name as that of the scale, called the KEY NOTE.

The G Major Scale

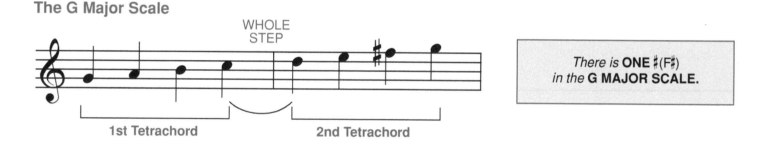

> There is **ONE** ♯ (F♯) *in the* **G MAJOR SCALE.**

The D Major Scale

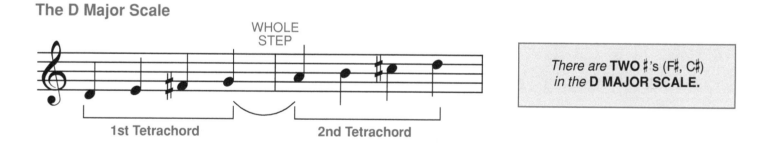

> There are **TWO** ♯'s (F♯, C♯) *in the* **D MAJOR SCALE.**

The A Major Scale

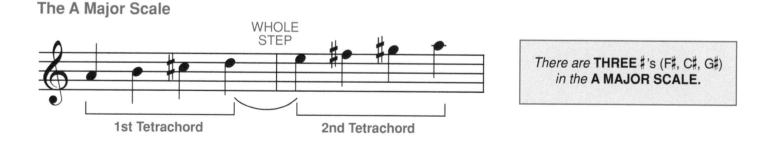

> There are **THREE** ♯'s (F♯, C♯, G♯) *in the* **A MAJOR SCALE.**

IMPORTANT!

The 2nd tetrachord of C is the 1st tetrachord of G.

The 2nd tetrachord of G is the 1st tetrachord of D.

The 2nd tetrachord of D is the 1st tetrachord of A.

The 2nd tetrachord of A is the 1st tetrachord of E.

This overlapping pattern will continue around the Circle of 5ths!

Triads

A TRIAD IS A 3-NOTE CHORD.

THE THREE NOTES OF A TRIAD ARE:

The ROOT is the note from which the triad gets its name. The ROOT of a C triad is C.

TRIADS MAY BE BUILT ON ANY NOTE OF ANY SCALE.

Root position triads in C

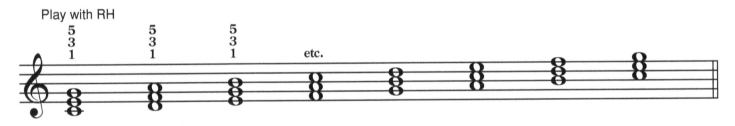

Triads: The 1st Inversion

ANY ROOT POSITION TRIAD MAY BE INVERTED BY MOVING THE ROOT TO THE TOP.

C E G **becomes** E G C

ALL LETTER NAMES ARE THE SAME, BUT THE ROOT IS ON TOP.
This is called the FIRST INVERSION.

1ST INVERSION TRIADS IN C

Play with RH. Use 1 2 5 on each triad.

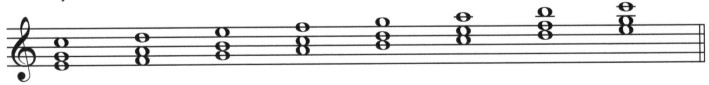

Play the above with LH ONE OCTAVE LOWER. Use 5 3 1 on each triad.

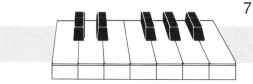

Triads: The 2nd Inversion

ANY 1st INVERSION TRIAD MAY BE INVERTED AGAIN
BY MOVING THE LOWEST NOTE TO THE TOP.

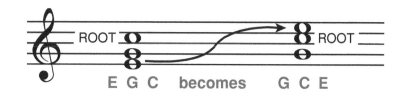

ALL LETTER NAMES ARE THE SAME, BUT THE ROOT IS IN THE MIDDLE.
This is called the SECOND INVERSION.

2ND INVERSION TRIADS IN C.

Play with RH. Use 1 3 5 on each triad.

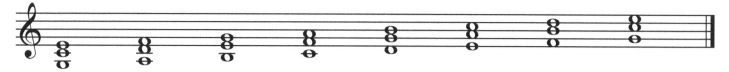

Play the above with LH ONE OCTAVE LOWER. Use 5 2 1 on each triad.

Triads in All Positions

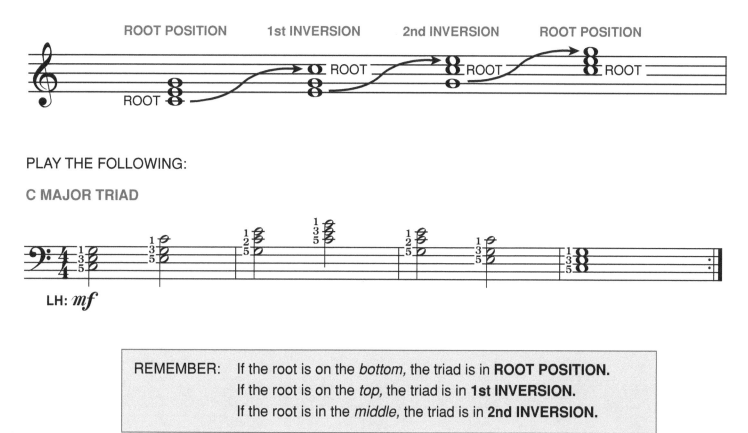

PLAY THE FOLLOWING:

C MAJOR TRIAD

LH: *mf*

REMEMBER: If the root is on the *bottom*, the triad is in **ROOT POSITION**.
If the root is on the *top*, the triad is in **1st INVERSION**.
If the root is in the *middle*, the triad is in **2nd INVERSION**.

The Primary Triads in Major Keys

The three most important triads in any key are those built on the 1st, 4th and 5th notes of the scale. These are called the **PRIMARY TRIADS** of the key.

The chords are identified by the Roman numerals, **I, IV** and **V** (1, 4 and 5).

In the key of C MAJOR, the **I CHORD** (1 chord) is the C TRIAD.
IV CHORD (4 chord) is the F TRIAD.
V CHORD (5 chord) is the G TRIAD.

The Primary Triads in C Major:

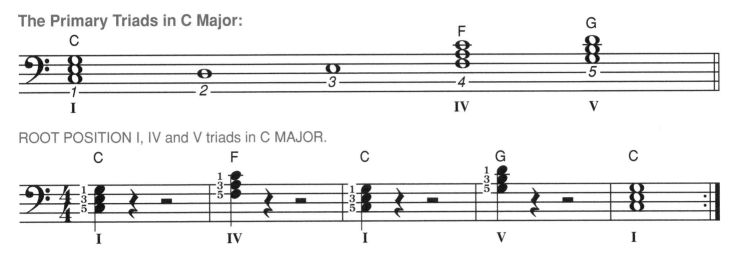

ROOT POSITION I, IV and V triads in C MAJOR.

Chord Progressions

When we change from one chord to another, we call this a "CHORD PROGRESSION."

When all chords are in root position, the hand must leap from one chord to the next when playing the primary triads.

To make the chord progressions easier to play and sound better, the IV and V chords may be played in other positions by moving one or more of the higher chord tones down an octave.

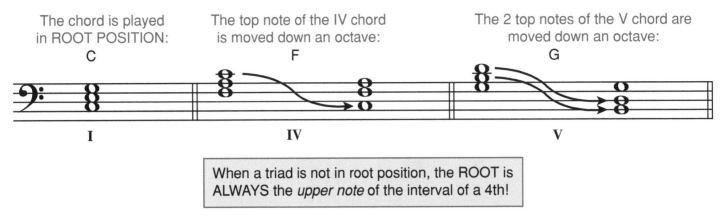

The chord is played in ROOT POSITION:

The top note of the IV chord is moved down an octave:

The 2 top notes of the V chord are moved down an octave:

When a triad is not in root position, the ROOT is ALWAYS the *upper note* of the interval of a 4th!

I, IV and V triads in C MAJOR. The following positions are often used for smooth progressions.

C Major Chord Progression with I, IV and V Chords. This chord progression is also called a cadence.

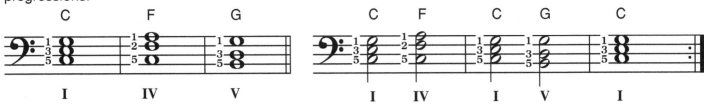

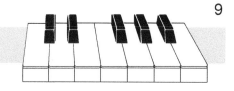

The V⁷ Chord

In many pieces a V7 CHORD is used instead of a V TRIAD.

To make a V7 chord, a note an interval of a 7th above the root is added to the V triad.

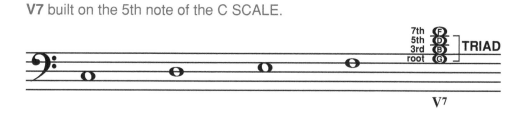

V7 built on the 5th note of the C SCALE.

To have a smoother and easier progression with the I and IV triads:

- The 5th (D) is omitted.
- The 3rd (B) and 7th (F) are moved down an octave.

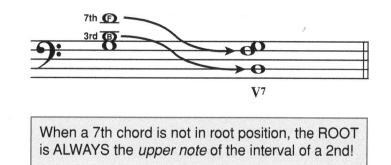

When a 7th chord is not in root position, the ROOT is ALWAYS the *upper note* of the interval of a 2nd!

The Primary Chords in C Major

The three PRIMARY CHORDS are now **I, IV** and **V7**.

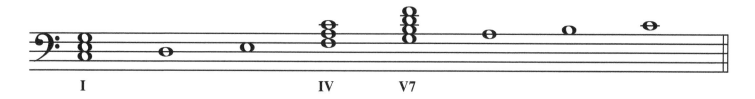

I IV V7

I, IV and V7 chords in C MAJOR. The following positions are often used for smoother progressions.

C Major Chord Progression with I, IV and V7 Chords.
This chord progression is also called a cadence.

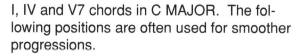

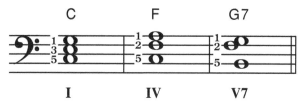

I IV V7

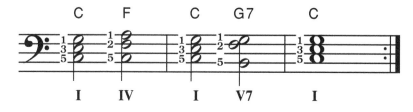

I IV I V7 I

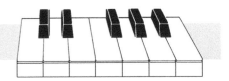

Scale Degrees

The tones of a scale are also called the *degrees* (or steps) of the scale. Each *scale degree* has a name.

THE 3 MOST IMPORTANT SCALE DEGREES: TONIC, DOMINANT and SUBDOMINANT.

The *key-note* (the tone of the same name as the scale) is called the **TONIC**. It is the lowest *and* highest tone of the scale.

The tone a 5th ABOVE the tonic is called the **DOMINANT**.

The tone a 5th BELOW the tonic is called the **SUBDOMINANT**.

SUB means "below" or "under" (SUBmarine, SUBway)

EACH SCALE DEGREE IS ALSO NUMBERED WITH A ROMAN NUMERAL WHICH IS DETERMINED BY ITS POSITION IN THE SCALE:

TONIC = I, DOMINANT = V, SUBDOMINANT = IV.

Important! The subdominant is numbered IV because of its position in the scale. It is called "subdominant" because it is the same distance BELOW the tonic as the dominant is ABOVE the tonic! It is NOT called "subdominant" because it is just below the dominant. See bottom music staff.

MORE SCALE DEGREES: MEDIANT and SUBMEDIANT

The tone a 3rd degree ABOVE the tonic (midway between the tonic and the dominant) is called the **MEDIANT**. Since the mediant is the 3rd degree of the scale, it is given the Roman numeral III.

The tone a 3rd degree BELOW the tonic (midway between the tonic and the subdominant) is called the **SUBMEDIANT**. Since the submediant is the 6th degree of the scale, it is given the Roman numeral VI.

Mediant is a Latin word meaning "in the middle."

FINAL SCALE DEGREES: SUPERTONIC and LEADING TONE

The tone a 2nd degree ABOVE the tonic is called the **SUPERTONIC**. Since the supertonic is the 2nd degree of the scale, it is given the Roman numeral II.

The tone a 2nd degree BELOW the tonic is called the **LEADING TONE**. The leading tone is sometimes called the SUBTONIC. Leading tone is most often used since the note has a strong tendency to "lead" to the TONIC, as it does in an ascending scale. Since the leading tone is the 7th degree of the scale, it is given the Roman numeral VII.

Note: The SUPERTONIC is always a WHOLE STEP above the tonic.
      The LEADING TONE is always a HALF STEP below the tonic.

You now know the names of all the scale degrees. Arranged in order the names are:

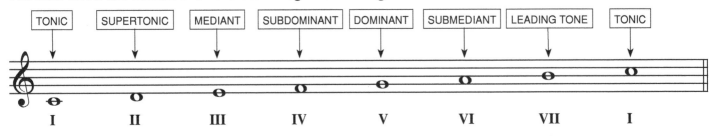

Be sure to remember that the degree names were derived from the following arrangement, in which the TONIC is taken as the center tone:

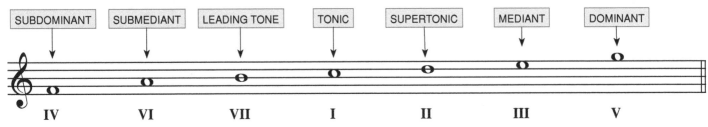

Arpeggios

The word ARPEGGIO comes from the Italian *arpeggiare*, which means "to play upon a harp." This refers to playing the notes of a chord in a broken fashion, one after another, as one does when playing a harp.

Arpeggios may be made from any chord. They may appear as simple broken chords or be in extended form, covering two or more octaves. However, only four kinds of chords are customarily studied as arpeggios: major and minor triads (in 3 positions) and the dominant 7th and diminished 7th chords (in 4 positions).

For more information on arpeggio fingering, see page 17.

Two-Octave Arpeggio

Hands together

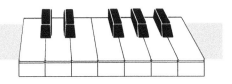

Building Minor Scales

Every MAJOR KEY has a RELATIVE MINOR KEY that has the same KEY SIGNATURE.
The RELATIVE MINOR begins on the 6th TONE of the MAJOR SCALE.

C Major Scale

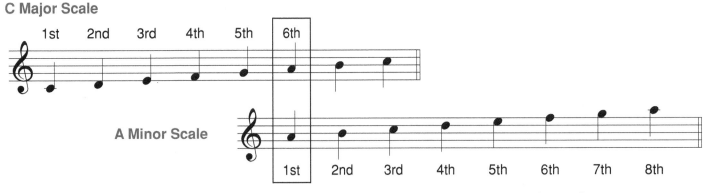

Because the keys of C MAJOR and A MINOR have the same KEY SIGNATURE (no #'s, no ♭'s),
they are relative.

The Key of A Minor (Relative of C Major)

THERE ARE THREE KINDS OF MINOR SCALES: the NATURAL, the HARMONIC and the MELODIC.

Play each of the following scales, first with the RH as written, then with the LH, 2 octaves lower than written.

1. **The Natural Minor Scale.**
   This scale uses *only* the tones of the relative minor scale.

2. **The Harmonic Minor Scale.**
   The 7th tone (G) is raised one half step, ASCENDING and DESCENDING.

3. **The Melodic Minor Scale.**
   In the ASCENDING SCALE, the 6th (F) and 7th (G) are raised one half step.
   The DESCENDING scale is the same as the natural minor.

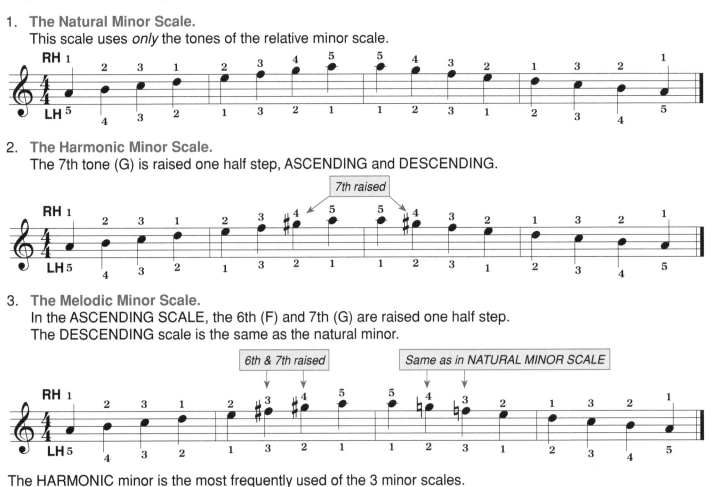

The HARMONIC minor is the most frequently used of the 3 minor scales.

To form a minor scale from any major scale of the same name, lower the following scale degrees ½ step.

	Ascending	Descending
Natural minor	3, 6, 7	3, 6, 7
Harmonic minor	3, 6	3, 6
Melodic minor	3	3, 6, 7

More About 3rds

Some 3rds are MAJOR 3rds, and some are MINOR (smaller) 3rds.

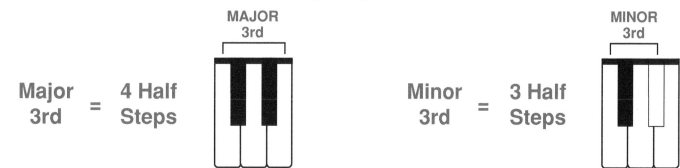

Major 3rd = **4 Half Steps**

Minor 3rd = **3 Half Steps**

ANY MAJOR 3rd MAY BE CHANGED TO A MINOR 3rd BY LOWERING THE UPPER NOTE ½ STEP!

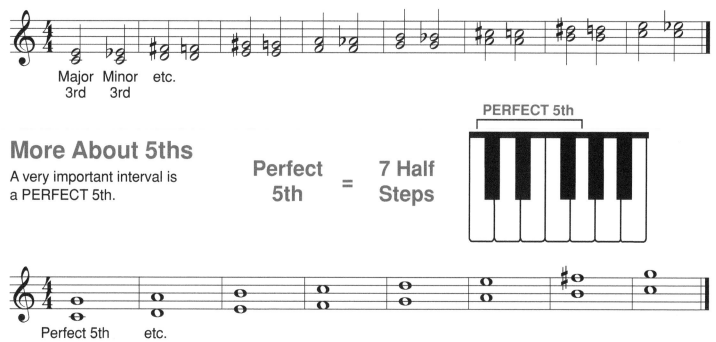

Major 3rd   Minor 3rd   etc.

More About 5ths

A very important interval is a PERFECT 5th.

Perfect 5th = **7 Half Steps**

Perfect 5th   etc.

More About Triads

MAJOR TRIADS consist of a ROOT, MAJOR 3rd and PERFECT 5th.

MINOR TRIADS consist of a ROOT, MINOR 3rd and PERFECT 5th.

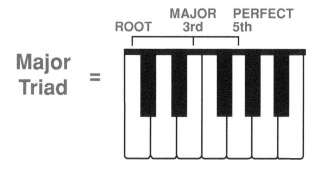

Major Triad =

Minor Triad =

ANY MAJOR TRIAD MAY BE CHANGED TO A MINOR TRIAD BY LOWERING THE 3rd ½ STEP!

Major Triad   Minor Triad   etc.

The Primary Triads in Minor Keys

To find the primary triads in a MINOR KEY, the HARMONIC MINOR SCALE is used.

In the A HARMONIC MINOR SCALE, the 7th note (G) is made SHARP, as an ACCIDENTAL.

Small lower case Roman numerals are used for the minor triads (i),
large upper case Roman numerals for major triads (V).

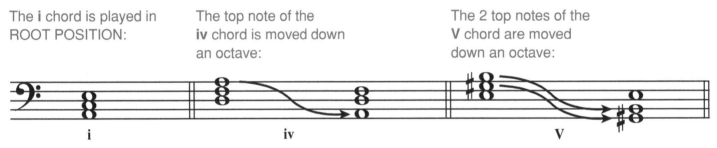

Notice that the i and iv chords are MINOR TRIADS. The V chord is a MAJOR TRIAD.
THIS IS TRUE IN ALL MINOR KEYS!

To make the chord progressions easier to play and sound better, the iv and V chords may be played in other positions by moving one or more of the higher chord tones down an octave.

The **i** chord is played in ROOT POSITION:

The top note of the **iv** chord is moved down an octave:

The 2 top notes of the **V** chord are moved down an octave:

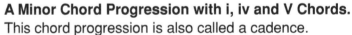

When a triad is not in root position, the ROOT is ALWAYS the *upper note* of the interval of a 4th!

The Primary Triads in A Minor

The i, iv and V triads in A minor:

A Minor Chord Progression with i, iv and V Chords.
This chord progression is also called a cadence.

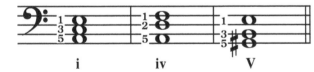

Using V7 instead of V
The V7 CHORD is made by adding a 7th to the V TRIAD.

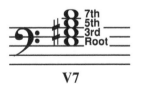

V7

To play the chord so it makes a smoother progression, omit the 5th, and move the 3rd and 7th down an octave.

V7

When a 7th chord is not in root position, the ROOT is ALWAYS the *upper note* of the interval of a 2nd!

The 3 PRIMARY CHORDS are now i, iv and V7. The following positions are often used for smooth progressions.

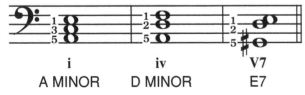

A Minor Chord Progressions with i, iv and V7 Chords.
This chord progression is also called a cadence.

The Diminished Seventh Chord

Remember: The DOMINANT SEVENTH CHORD may be formed by adding one note to the major triad, a minor 3rd above the 5th.

The DIMINISHED SEVENTH CHORD may be formed by lowering each note of the DOMINANT SEVENTH chord (V^7) 1 half step, except for the root, which remains the same.

C DOMINANT 7th (C7)

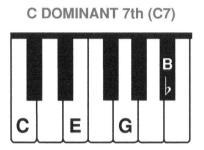

C DIMINISHED 7th (Cdim7)

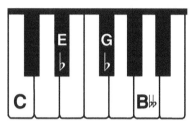

Listed below are dominant 7th and diminished 7th chords for you to compare. Notice that when lowering the notes of the dominant 7th chord to form the diminished 7th chord, the note name remains the same. The B♭ becomes B♭♭ (B double-flat), not A.

DOMINANT 7ths				DIMINISHED 7ths			
Root	3rd	5th	7th	Root	3rd	5th	7th
D	F♯	A	C	D	F	A♭	C♭
G	B	D	F	G	B♭	D♭	F♭
C	E	G	B♭	C	E♭	G♭	B♭♭
F	A	C	E♭	F	A♭	C♭	E♭♭
B♭	D	F	A♭	B♭	D♭	F♭	A♭♭
E♭	G	B♭	D♭	E♭	G♭	B♭♭	D♭♭
A♭	C	E♭	G♭	A♭	C♭	E♭♭	G♭♭

A DIMINISHED SEVENTH CHORD may also be formed on any given root by skipping the interval of a MINOR 3rd (3 HALF STEPS) between each note.

Play the following DOMINANT 7th and DIMINISHED 7th chords.

Guide to Fingering

While it is probably easier to internalize scale and arpeggio fingerings through repetition than to memorize a list of rules, the following may be of some value to certain pianists. Fingering is a very personal affair. The span of your hand, the stretch between your fingers and your own personal preference will determine how best to finger each passage. Nevertheless, the following fingering has been generally decided to be the most comfortable for most pianists.

Major and Harmonic Minor Scales

1. On this page and the scale pages that follow, fingering in ( ) is optional and should be used when continuing upward or downward for 2 or more octaves.

2. Fingering for All Major Scales

A. *Beginning on White Keys*
With two exceptions, the ascending RH fingering and the descending LH fingering for all major scales beginning on a white key is: 1 2 3 1 - 2 3 4 5. When playing scales for more than one octave, use RH 1 on the octave note. The 5th finger is used only to end a scale in the RH, or begin a scale in the LH.

> The two exceptions are F major for the RH: 1 2 3 4 – 1 2 3 4 (ascending).
> B major for the LH: 1 2 3 4 – 1 2 3 4 (descending).

B. *Beginning on Black Keys for the RH*
The starting RH finger for all major scales beginning on a black key is 2. You may also begin these scales with the finger that ends the scale. This ending finger is the beginning finger for the next octave when playing for two or more octaves—2 and 3 on the 2-black key group, 2, 3 and 4 on the 3-black key group.

> C♯/D♭: 2 3 1 2 – 3 4 1 2. Begin with 2.
> E♭: 2 1 2 3 – 4 1 2 3. May begin with 3.
>
> F♯/G♭: 2 3 4 1 – 2 3 1 2. Begin with 2.
> A♭: 2 3 1 2 – 3 1 2 3. May begin with 3.
> B♭: 2 1 2 3 – 1 2 3 4. May begin with 4.

C. *Beginning on Black Keys for the LH*
With one exception, the starting LH finger for all major scales beginning on a black key is 3—the exception is F♯/G♭ which starts with a 4. The ending finger is generally 2, but you may also end these scales with the finger that begins the scale. This ending finger is the beginning finger for the next octave when playing for two or more octaves.

The fingering in ascending order is:

> C♯/D♭: 3 2 1 4 – 3 2 1 2. May end with 3.
> E♭: 3 2 1 4 – 3 2 1 2. May end with 3.*
>
> F♯/G♭: 4 3 2 1 – 3 2 1 2. May end with 4.
> A♭: 3 2 1 4 – 3 2 1 2. May end with 3.
> B♭: 3 2 1 4 – 3 2 1 2. May end with 3.

*Only the descending LH in the E♭ major scale is fingered the same way as the ascending RH — in all other scales beginning on a black key, the fingerings are different.

3. With just a few exceptions, the major scale and its parallel harmonic minor are fingered the same (C major - C harmonic minor; G major - G harmonic minor, etc.).

The fingering in which the harmonic minor is *different* than its parallel major is:

> RH in F♯ and C♯ minors: 2 3 1 2 – 3 1 2 3 (may begin with 3 4).
> LH in A♯ minor: 2 1 3 2 – 1 4 3 2.
> LH in E♭ minor: 2 1 4 3 – 2 1 3 2.

4. The 4th finger is usually used only once in an octave. The 4th finger is important because if you know the position of the 4th finger, you can figure out the position of the other fingers. Because of this, the 4th finger of each hand and the degree of the scale it falls on is shown at the top of the scale pages that follow for each major and minor scale. When there is an exception it is so noted just above the music.

The following guide gives the position of the 4th finger in all major scales and their parallel harmonic minors.

> **Group A.** The C scale plus all major scales with up to 4 sharps:
> The keys of C, G, D, A, E (and F, LH only).
>
> RH: 4th finger on the 7th degree
> LH: 4th finger on the 2nd degree (includes F scales).

> **Group B.** All major scales with up to 4 flats:
> The keys of F (RH only), B♭, E♭, A♭.
>
> RH: 4th finger on B♭. In the 1st octave, however,
> B♭ major may use 2 (or 4) on the first B♭, 4 thereafter.
> A♭ major may use 3 (or 4) on the first B♭, 4 thereafter.
>
> LH: 4th finger on the 4th degree
> except for the F scales — see Group A, above, and the
> B♭ & E♭ harmonic minors — 4th finger on G♭.

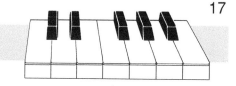

Group C. All major scales using 5 black keys:
The keys of B/C♭, F♯/G♭, C♯/D♭.

RH: 4th finger on A♯/B♭. In the 1st octave, however,
C♯ minor uses 3 (or 4) on the first D♯, 4 thereafter.
F♯ minor uses 3 (or 4) on the first G♯, 4 thereafter.
G♯ minor uses 3 (or 4) on the first A♯, 4 thereafter.

LH: 4th finger on F♯ (G♭).
In the 1st octave, however,
B major also uses 4 on the first B, 1 thereafter.

Arpeggios

The difficulties in fingering triad arpeggios successfully (major, minor, & all inversions) are slight when compared to scale playing. The chief concern is the proper use of the 3rd and 4th fingers when playing arpeggios containing only white keys. There are two fingerings for each hand to choose from:
LH 5 – 4 – 2 – 1 or 5 – 3 – 2 – 1 and RH 1 – 2 – 3 – 5 or 1 – 2 – 4 – 5.

The general rule is:
when the distance between the 2 lower notes in the LH and the 2 higher notes in the RH is a **4th** (5 half-steps), use the **3rd** finger (LH 5 – 3, RH 3 – 5);
when the distance is a **3rd** (3 or 4 half-steps), use the **4th** finger (LH 5 – 4,* RH 4 – 5).

Major Key Arpeggios
ROOT POSITION
RH fingering for most keys: 1 – 2 – 3 – 1 and ending with 5.
Exceptions are the keys of B♭, E♭, A♭, C♯/D♭: 2 (4) – 1 – 2 – 4.**

LH fingering in the keys of C, G, F: 5 – 4 – 2 – 1.*
in the keys of D, A, E, B/C♭, F♯/G♭: 5 – 3 – 2 – 1.
in the keys of E♭, A♭, C♯/D♭: 2 – 1 – 4 – 2.
in the key of B♭: 3 – 2 – 1 – 3.

Minor Key Arpeggios
ROOT POSITION
RH fingering for most keys: 1 – 2 – 3 – 1 and ending with 5.
Exceptions are the keys of F♯, C♯, G♯/A♭: 2 (4) – 1 – 2 – 4,**
and A♯/B♭: 2 – 3 – 1 – 2.

LH fingering for most keys: 5 – 4 – 2 – 1.*
Exceptions are the keys of F♯, C♯, G♯/A♭: 2 – 1 – 4 – 2,
and A♯/B♭: 3 – 2 – 1 – 3.

*Though the above LH fingering is the one used by most pianists, there are those who prefer the fingering 5 – 3 – 2 – 1. The preference seems to be determined by the pianist's span between the 5th, 4th and 3rd fingers and the larger stretch for the 4th finger crossing over the thumb in the two octave arpeggio.

**Fingering in ( ) is optional and should be used when continuing upward or downward for 2 or more octaves.

Chromatic Scales

The fingering for the chromatic scale is much simpler than that for either the major or the minor scales. Because of the elevated position of the hand required to perform this scale and the short distance covered in passing the thumb under, it may be played with great smoothness and speed with only slight difficulty. The first fingering listed below is the most widely used.

1. RH: 1 on all white keys except C (2) and F (2). You may begin with 1 on C, if you prefer.
    LH: 1 on all white keys except B (2) and E (2). You may begin with 4 on C, if you prefer.
    Both hands: 3 on all black keys.

2. Same as above, except that
    RH: 1, 2, 3, 4 fall in succession on G, G♯, A, A♯ (ascending).
    LH: 4, 3, 2, 1 fall in succession on F♯, G, G♯, A (ascending).

Key of C Major
Major Scales

LH: 4th finger on D (2nd degree of scale). **RH:** 4th finger on B (7th degree of scale).*

Parallel motion in octaves.

Contrary motion starting on the same note.

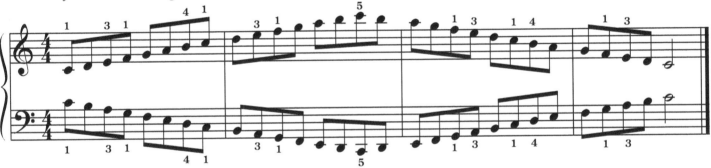

Parallel motion in thirds or tenths.

Parallel motion in sixths.

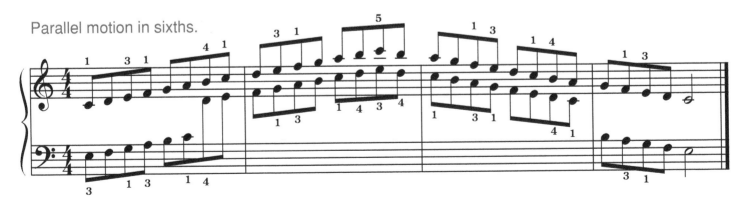

*For the importance of knowing the position of the 4th finger, see page 16, par. 4.

C Major Triads Root position

*For more information on arpeggio fingering, see page 17.

Key of G Major
Major Scales

LH: 4th finger on A (2nd degree). **RH:** 4th finger on F♯ (7th degree).

Parallel motion in octaves.

Contrary motion starting on the same note.

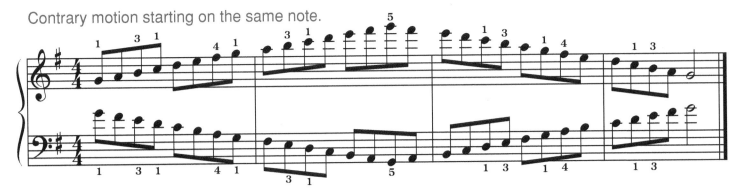

Parallel motion in thirds or tenths.

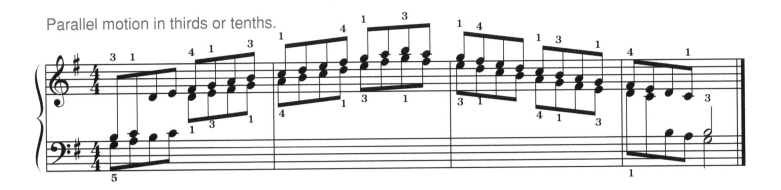

Parallel motion in sixths.

G Major Triads Root position

Key of D Major
Major Scales

LH: 4th finger on E (2nd degree).   RH: 4th finger on C♯ (7th degree).

Parallel motion in octaves.

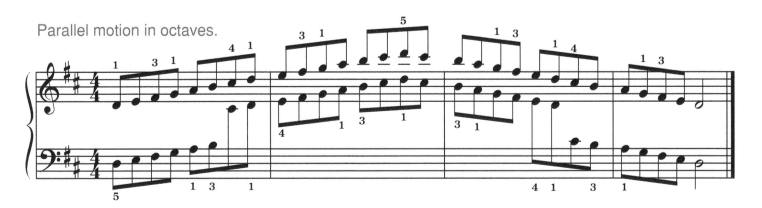

Contrary motion starting on the same note.

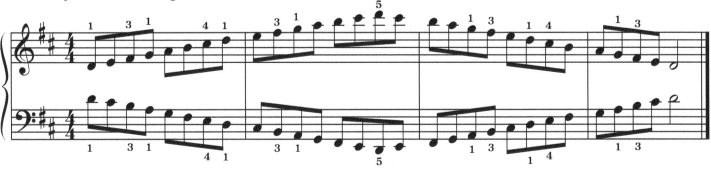

Parallel motion in thirds or tenths.

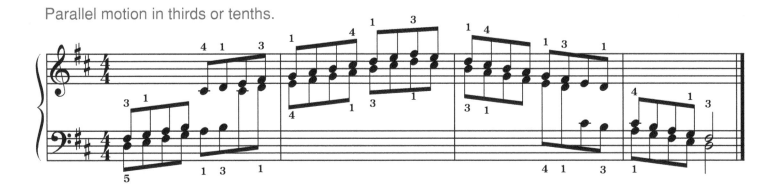

Parallel motion in sixths.

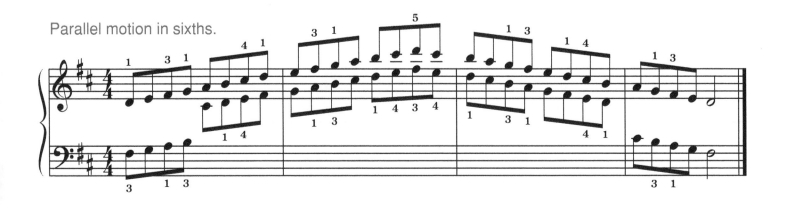

D Major Triads Root position

tonic   supertonic   mediant   subdominant   dominant   submediant   leading tone   tonic

D Major Cadences Three Positions

D Major Arpeggios Two-octave arpeggios

Dominant Seventh Arpeggios Two-octave arpeggios

5

Key of A Major
Major Scales

LH: 4th finger on B (2nd degree). **RH:** 4th finger on G♯ (7th degree).

Parallel motion in octaves.

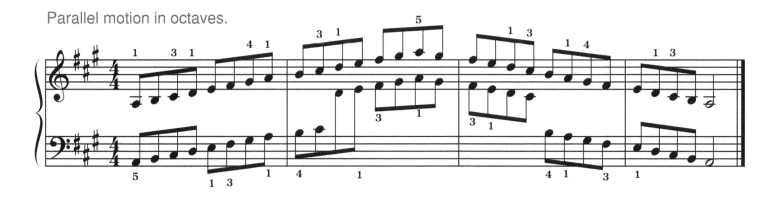

Contrary motion starting on the same note.

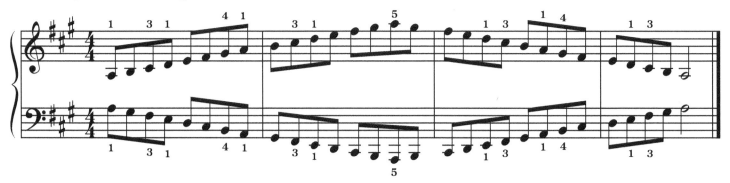

Parallel motion in thirds or tenths.

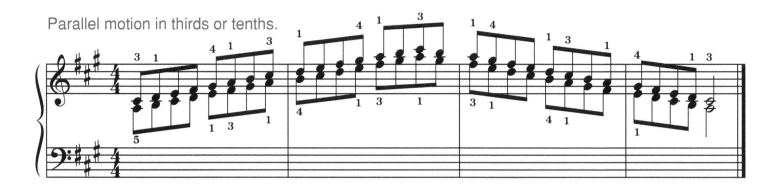

Parallel motion in sixths.

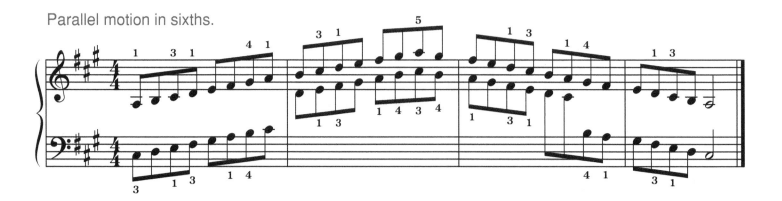

A Major Triads Root position

Key of E Major
Major Scales

LH: 4th finger on F♯ (2nd degree). RH: 4th finger on D♯ (7th degree).

Parallel motion in octaves.

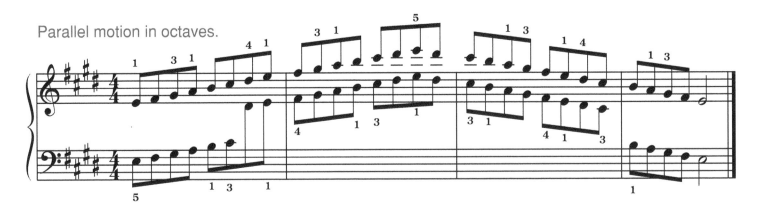

Contrary motion starting on the same note.

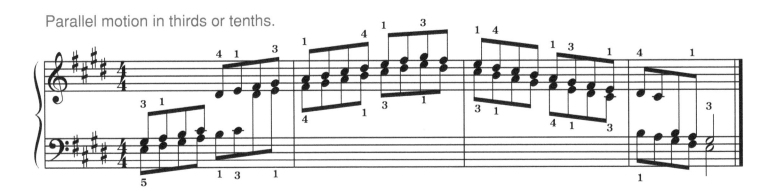

Parallel motion in thirds or tenths.

Parallel motion in sixths.

Key of B Major*
Major Scales

LH: 4th finger on B and F♯ (1st and 5th degrees).** **RH:** 4th finger on A♯ (7th degree).

Parallel motion in octaves.

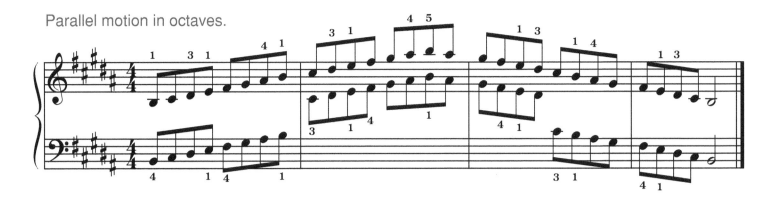

Contrary motion starting on the same note.

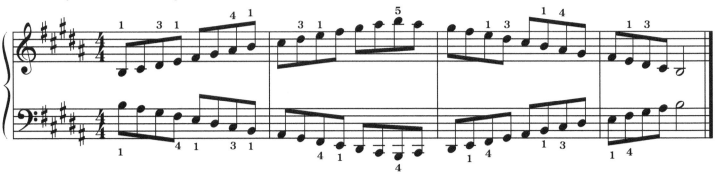

Parallel motion in thirds or tenths.

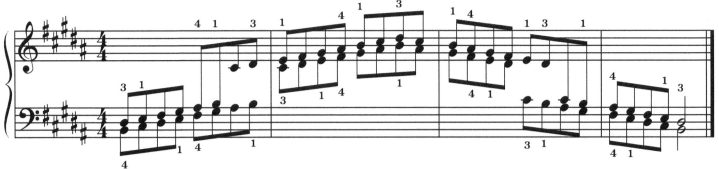

Parallel motion in sixths.

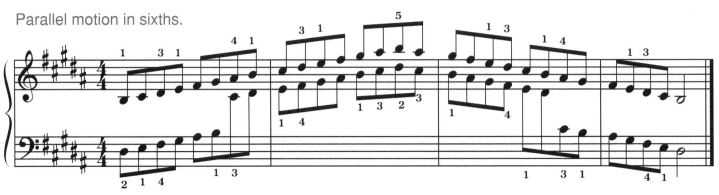

*Enharmonic with C♭ major. See page 46.
**In the 1st octave, LH 4 is used on B—LH 1 thereafter.

B Major Triads Root position

Primary Chords

B   C#m   D#m   E   F#   G#m   A#dim   B   B   E   F# or F#7

I   ii   iii   IV   V   vi   vii°   I   I   IV   V or V7

tonic supertonic mediant subdominant dominant submediant leading tone tonic

B Major Cadences Three Positions

I   IV   I   V or V7   I   I   IV   I   V or V7   I   I   IV   I   V or V7   I

B Major Arpeggios Two-octave arpeggios

root position   1st inversion   2nd inversion

Dominant Seventh Arpeggios Two-octave arpeggios

root position   1st inversion

2nd inversion   3rd inversion

Key of F♯ Major*

Major Scales

LH: 4th finger on F♯ (1st degree). **RH:** 4th finger on A♯ (3rd degree).

Parallel motion in octaves.

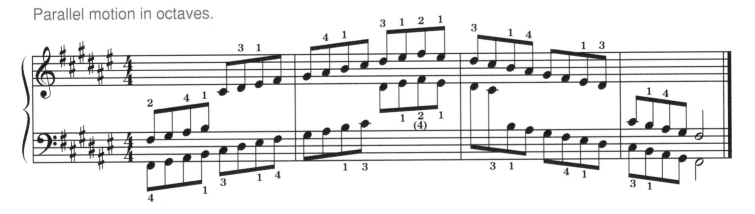

Contrary motion starting on the same note.

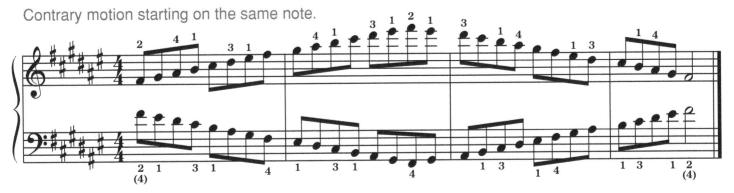

Parallel motion in thirds or tenths.

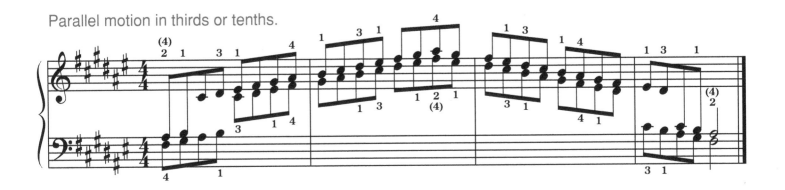

Parallel motion in sixths.

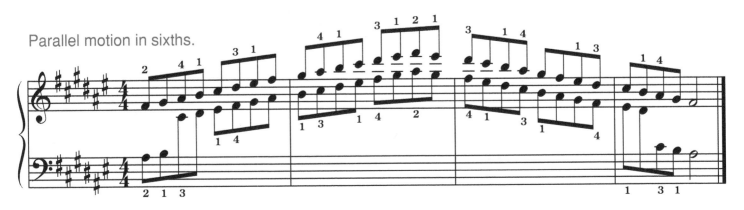

*Enharmonic with G♭ major. See page 44.

Key of C♯ Major*
Major Scales

LH: 4th finger on F♯ (4th degree). **RH:** 4th finger on A♯(6th degree).

Parallel motion in octaves.

Contrary motion starting on the same note.

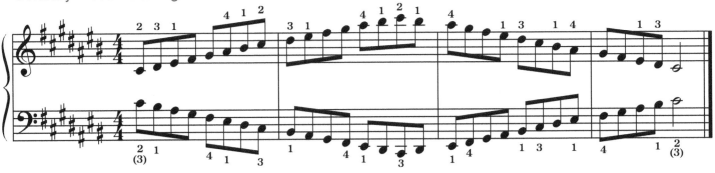

Parallel motion in thirds or tenths.

Parallel motion in sixths.

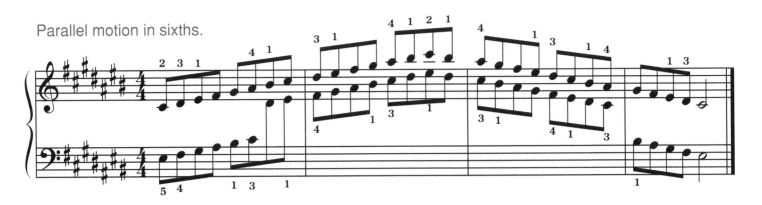

*Enharmonic with D♭ major. See page 42.

C♯ Major Triads Root position

⌐ Primary Chords ⌐

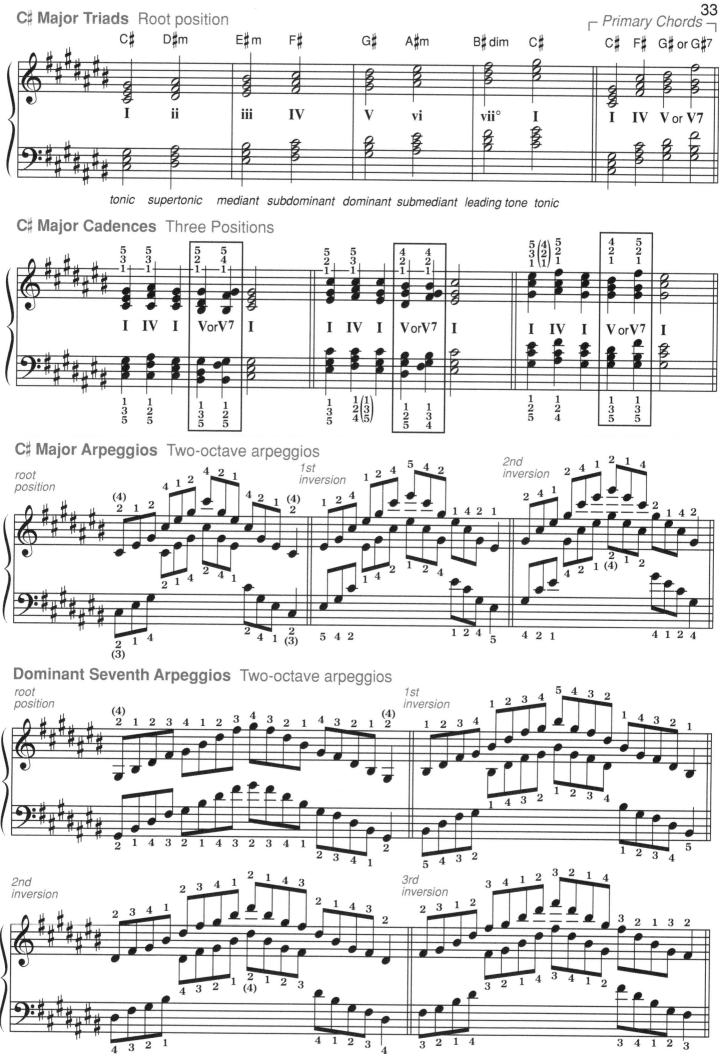

C♯   D♯m   E♯m   F♯   G♯   A♯m   B♯dim   C♯   C♯   F♯   G♯ or G♯7

I   ii   iii   IV   V   vi   vii°   I   I   IV   V or V7

tonic   supertonic   mediant   subdominant   dominant   submediant   leading tone   tonic

C♯ Major Cadences Three Positions

I   IV   I   V or V7   I   I   IV   I   V or V7   I   I   IV   I   V or V7   I

C♯ Major Arpeggios Two-octave arpeggios

root position

1st inversion

2nd inversion

Dominant Seventh Arpeggios Two-octave arpeggios

root position

1st inversion

2nd inversion

3rd inversion

Part 3

Key of F Major
Major Scales

LH: 4th finger on G (2nd degree of scale). **RH:** 4th finger on B♭ (4th degree of scale).*

Parallel motion in octaves.

Contrary motion starting on the same note.

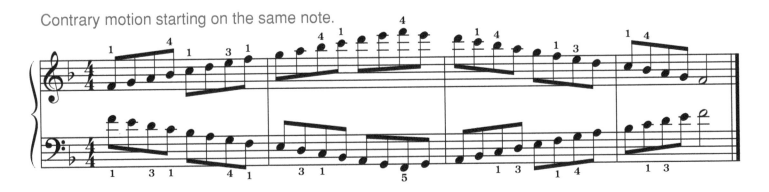

Parallel motion in thirds or tenths.

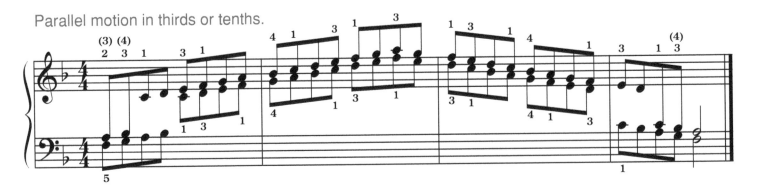

Parallel motion in sixths.

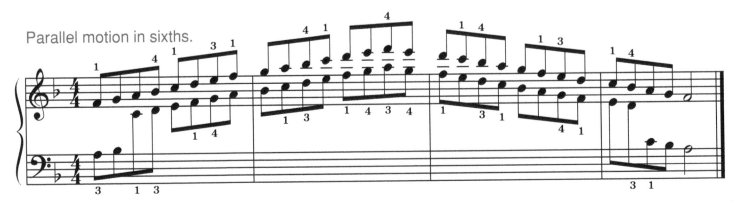

*For the importance of knowing the position of the 4th finger, see page 16, par. 4.

F Major Triads Root position

tonic   supertonic   mediant   subdominant   dominant   submediant   leading tone   tonic

F Major Cadences Three Positions

F Major Arpeggios Two-octave arpeggios

Dominant Seventh Arpeggios Two-octave arpeggios

Key of B♭ Major
Major Scales

LH: 4th finger on E♭ (4th degree). **RH:** 4th finger on B♭ (1st degree).*

Parallel motion in octaves.

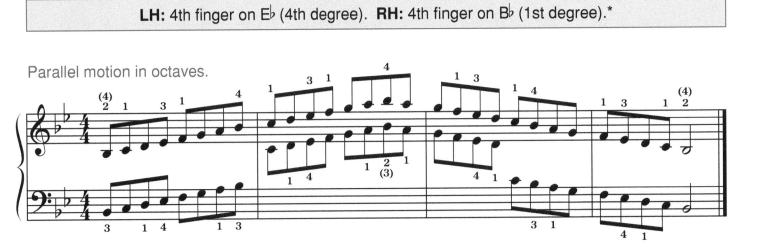

Contrary motion starting on the same note.

Parallel motion in thirds or tenths.

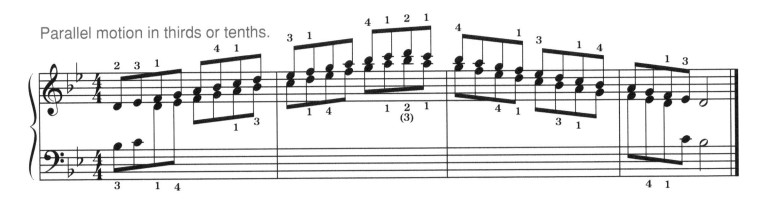

Parallel motion in sixths.

*In the 1st octave, RH 2 or 4 may be used on B♭—RH 4 thereafter.

B♭ Major Triads Root position

Primary Chords

B♭ Cm Dm E♭ F Gm A dim B♭   B♭ E♭ F or F7

I ii iii IV V vi vii° I   I IV V or V7

tonic supertonic mediant subdominant dominant submediant leading tone tonic

B♭ Major Cadences Three Positions

I IV I V or V7 I   I IV I V or V7 I   I IV I V or V7 I

B♭ Major Arpeggios Two-octave arpeggios

root position

1st inversion

2nd inversion

Dominant Seventh Arpeggios Two-octave arpeggios

root position

1st inversion

2nd inversion

3rd inversion

Key of E♭ Major
Major Scales

LH: 4th finger on A♭ (4th degree). **RH:** 4th finger on B♭ (5th degree).

Parallel motion in octaves.

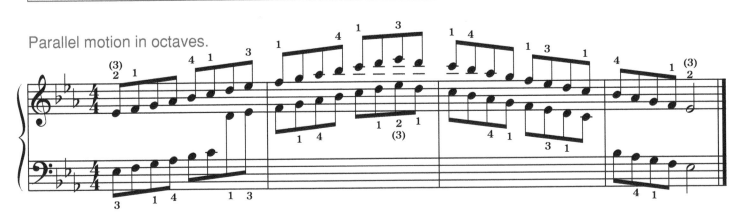

Contrary motion starting on the same note.

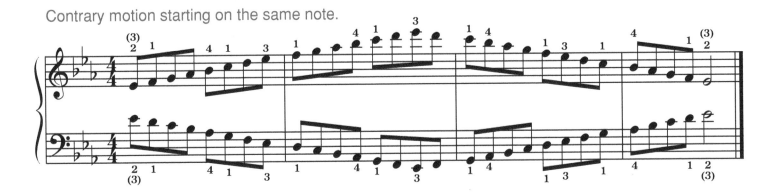

Parallel motion in thirds or tenths.

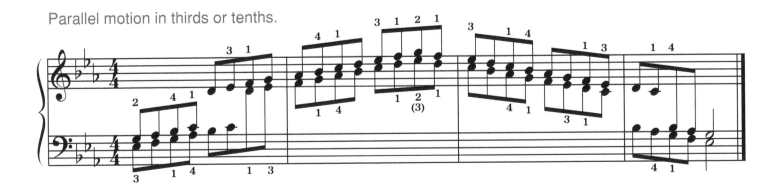

Parallel motion in sixths.

E♭ Major Triads Root position

Primary Chords

tonic   supertonic   mediant   subdominant   dominant   submediant   leading tone   tonic

E♭ Major Cadences Three Positions

E♭ Major Arpeggios Two-octave arpeggios

Dominant Seventh Arpeggios Two-octave arpeggios

Key of A♭ Major
Major Scales

LH: 4th finger on D♭ (4th degree). **RH:** 4th finger on B♭ (2nd degree).*

Parallel motion in octaves.

Contrary motion starting on the same note.

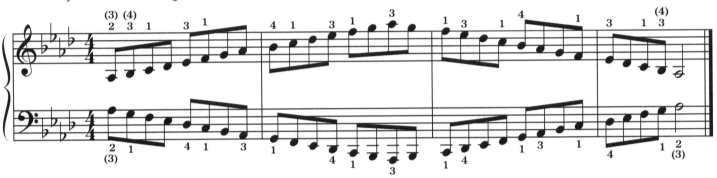

Parallel motion in thirds or tenths.

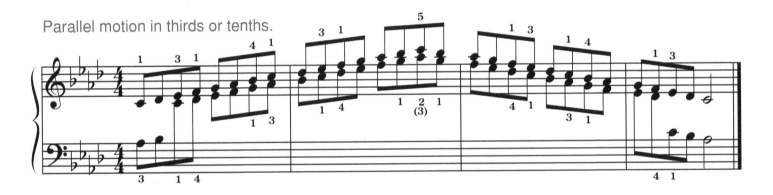

Parallel motion in sixths.

*In the 1st octave, RH 3 or 4 may be used on B♭—RH 4 thereafter.

A♭ Major Triads Root position

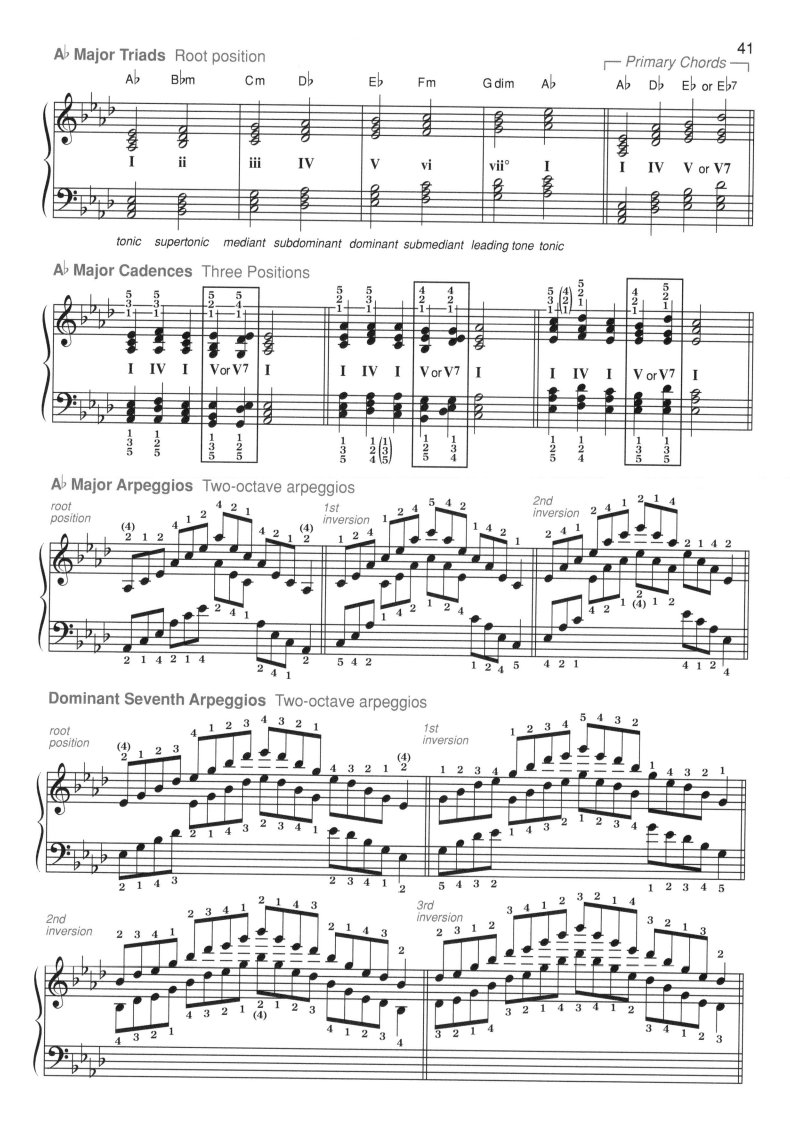

Primary Chords

A♭	B♭m	Cm	D♭	E♭	Fm	G dim	A♭	A♭	D♭	E♭ or E♭7
I	ii	iii	IV	V	vi	vii°	I	I	IV	V or V7

tonic   supertonic   mediant   subdominant   dominant   submediant   leading tone   tonic

A♭ Major Cadences Three Positions

I	IV	I	V or V7	I	I	IV	I	V or V7	I	I	IV	I	V or V7	I

A♭ Major Arpeggios Two-octave arpeggios

root position   1st inversion   2nd inversion

Dominant Seventh Arpeggios Two-octave arpeggios

root position   1st inversion

2nd inversion   3rd inversion

Key of D♭ Major*

Major Scales

LH: 4th finger on G♭ (4th degree). **RH:** 4th finger on B♭ (6th degree).

Parallel motion in octaves.

Contrary motion starting on the same note.

Parallel motion in thirds or tenths.

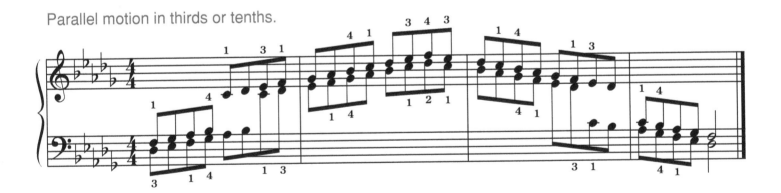

Parallel motion in sixths.

*Enharmonic with C♯ major. See page 32.

D♭ Major Triads Root position

tonic   supertonic   mediant   subdominant   dominant   submediant   leading tone   tonic

D♭ Major Cadences Three Positions

D♭ Major Arpeggios Two-octave arpeggios

Dominant Seventh Arpeggios Two-octave arpeggios

Key of G♭ Major*
Major Scales

LH: 4th finger on G♭ (1st degree). **RH:** 4th finger on B♭ (3rd degree).

Parallel motion in octaves.

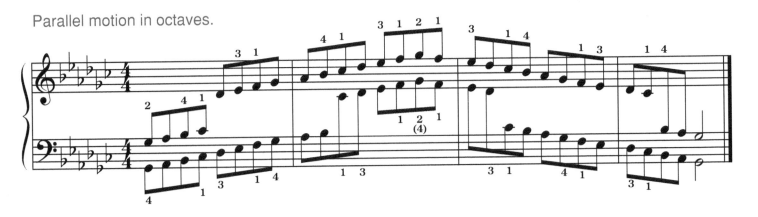

Contrary motion starting on the same note.

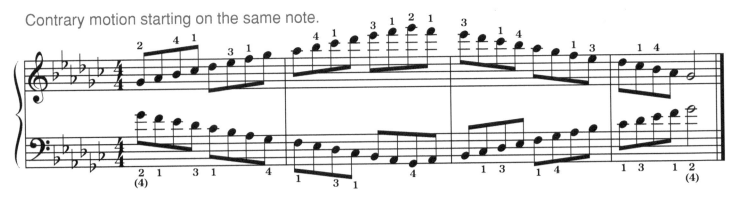

Parallel motion in thirds or tenths.

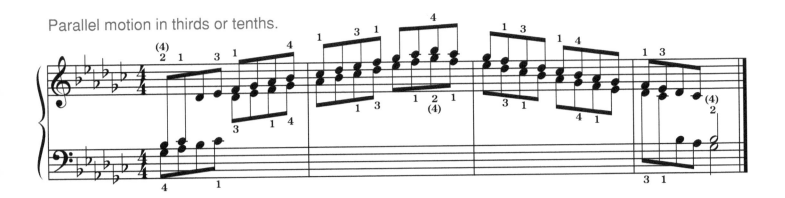

Parallel motion in sixths.

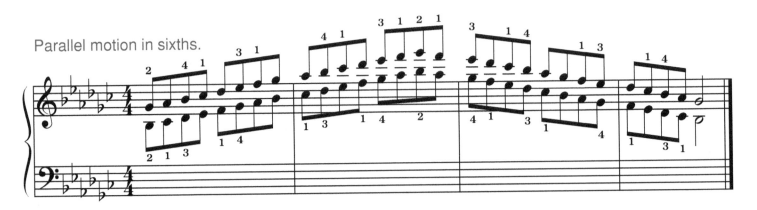

*Enharmonic with F♯ major. See page 30.

Gb **Major Triads** Root position

Primary Chords

Gb Major Cadences Three Positions

Gb Major Arpeggios Two-octave arpeggios

Dominant Seventh Arpeggios Two-octave arpeggios

Key of C♭ Major*
Major Scales

LH: 4th finger on C♭ and G♭ (1st and 5th degrees).** **RH:** 4th finger on B♭ (7th degree).

Parallel motion in octaves.

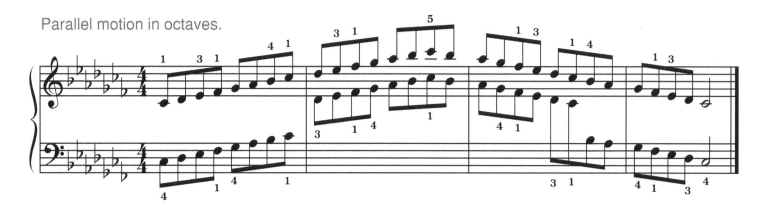

Contrary motion starting on the same note.

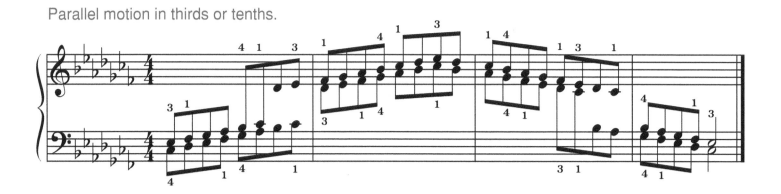

Parallel motion in thirds or tenths.

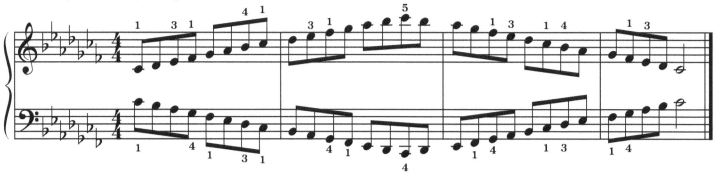

Parallel motion in sixths.

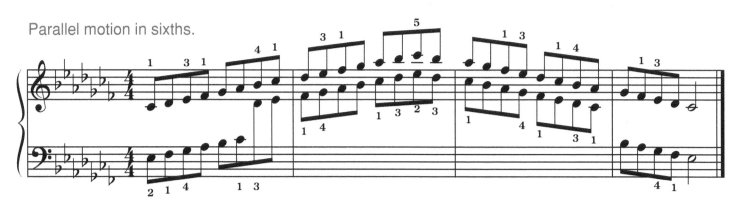

*Enharmonic with B major. See page 28.

**In the 1st octave, LH 4 is used on C♭—LH 1 thereafter.

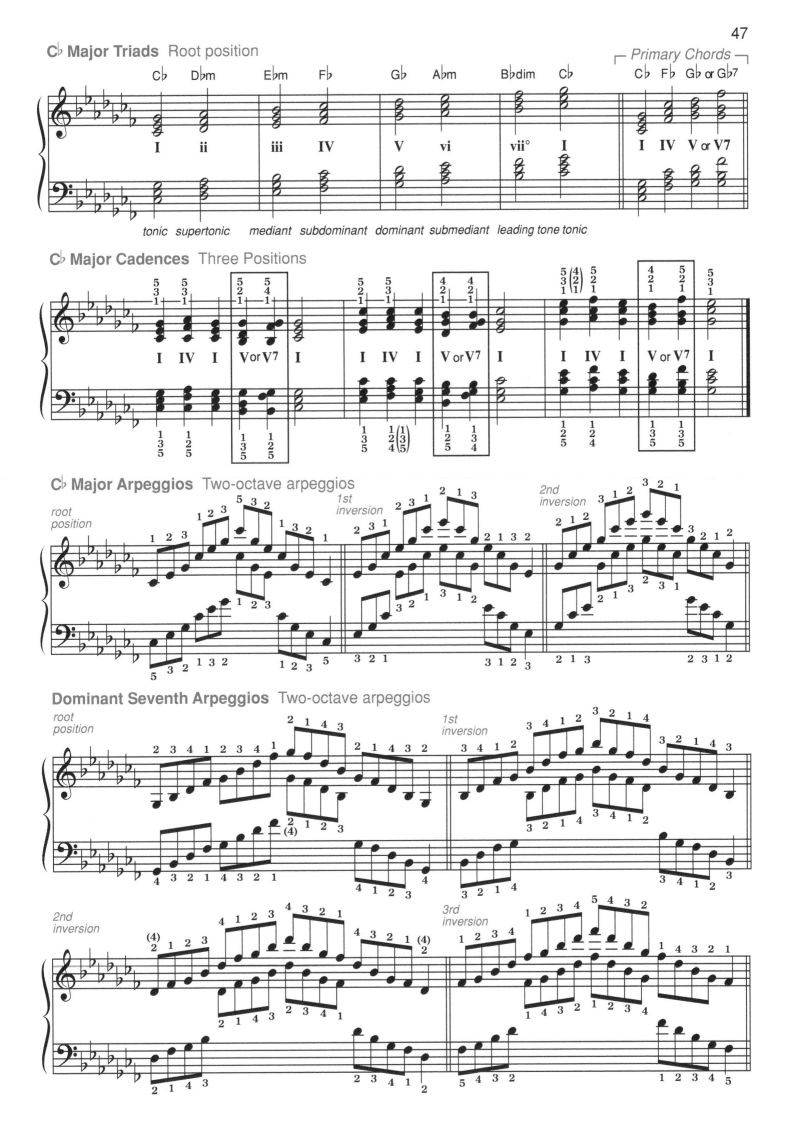

C♭ **Major Triads** Root position

tonic supertonic mediant subdominant dominant submediant leading tone tonic

C♭ **Major Cadences** Three Positions

C♭ **Major Arpeggios** Two-octave arpeggios

Dominant Seventh Arpeggios Two-octave arpeggios

Key of A Minor
Relative Minor of C Major

> **LH:** 4th finger on B (2nd degree of scale).   **RH:** 4th finger on G or G♯ (7th degree of scale).*

Natural minor scale, parallel motion in octaves.

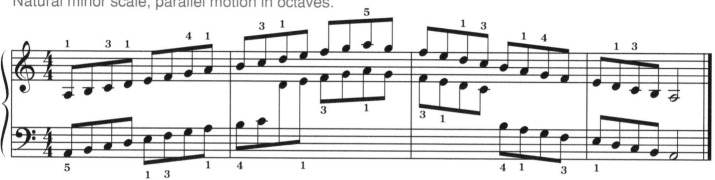

Harmonic minor scale, parallel motion in octaves.

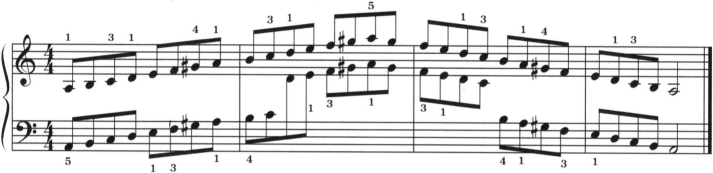

Harmonic minor scale, contrary motion.

Melodic minor scale, parallel motion in octaves. RH 4th finger on G♯ ascending, G♮ descending.

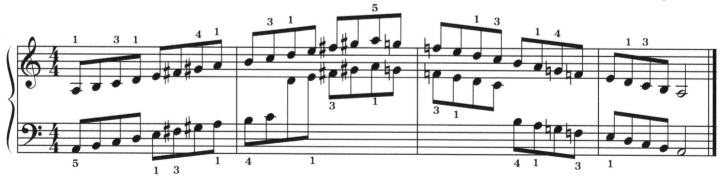

*For the importance of knowing the position of the 4th finger, see page 16, par. 4.

A Minor Triads Root position

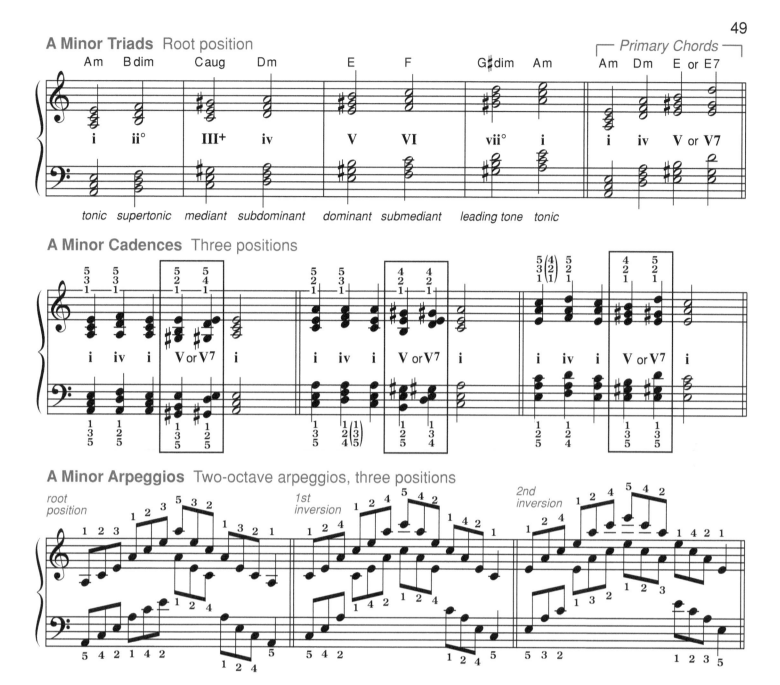

Am Bdim Caug Dm E F G♯dim Am ⌐ Primary Chords ⌐ Am Dm E or E7

i ii° III+ iv V VI vii° i i iv V or V7

tonic supertonic mediant subdominant dominant submediant leading tone tonic

A Minor Cadences Three positions

i iv i V or V7 i   i iv i V or V7 i   i iv i V or V7 i

A Minor Arpeggios Two-octave arpeggios, three positions

root position   1st inversion   2nd inversion

Diminished Seventh Arpeggios Two-octave arpeggios, four positions

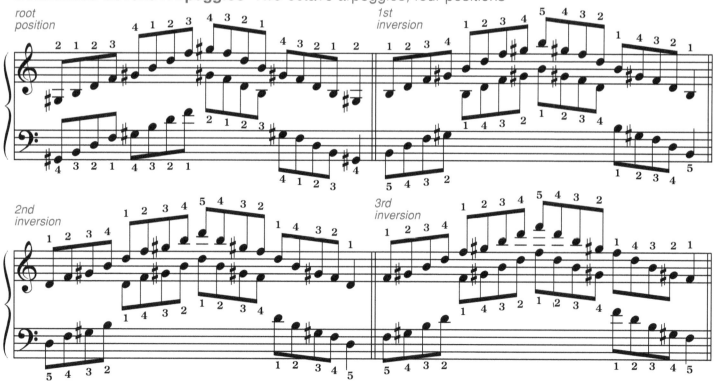

root position   1st inversion

2nd inversion   3rd inversion

Key of E Minor

Relative Minor of G Major

LH: 4th finger on F♯ (2nd degree). **RH:** 4th finger on D or D♯ (7th degree).

Natural minor scale, parallel motion in octaves.

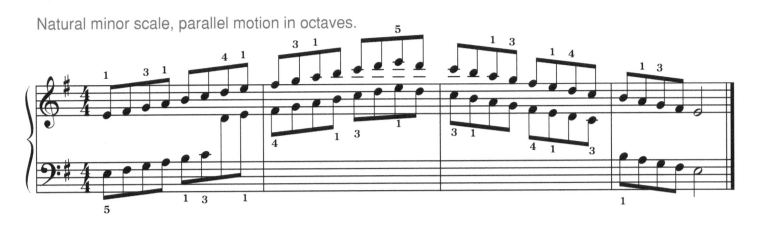

Harmonic minor scale, parallel motion in octaves.

Harmonic minor scale, contrary motion.

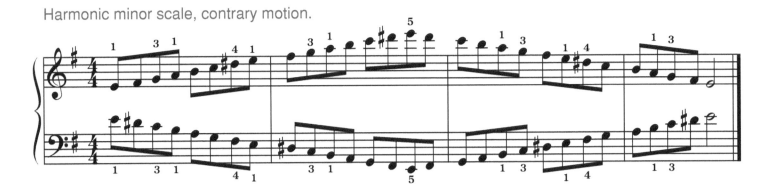

Melodic minor scale, parallel motion in octaves. RH 4th finger on D♯ ascending, D♮ descending.

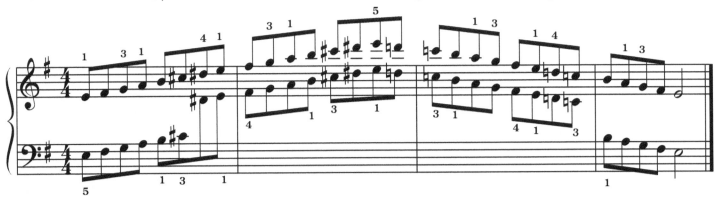

Key of B Minor
Relative Minor of D Major

LH: 4th finger on B and F♯ (1st and 5th degrees).*   **RH:** 4th finger on A or A♯ (7th degree).

Natural minor scale, parallel motion in octaves.

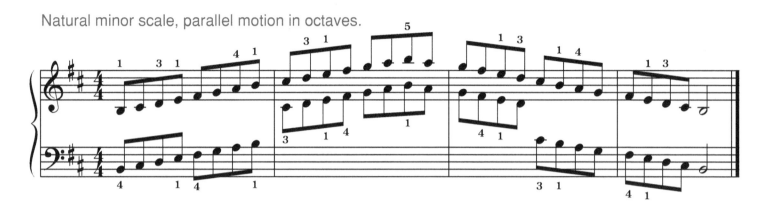

Harmonic minor scale, parallel motion in octaves.

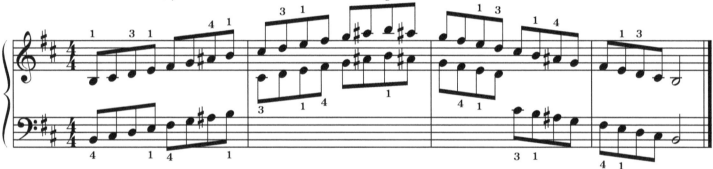

Harmonic minor scale, contrary motion.

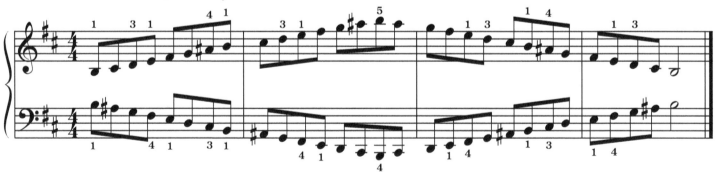

Melodic minor scale, parallel motion in octaves. RH 4th finger on A♯ ascending, A♮ descending.

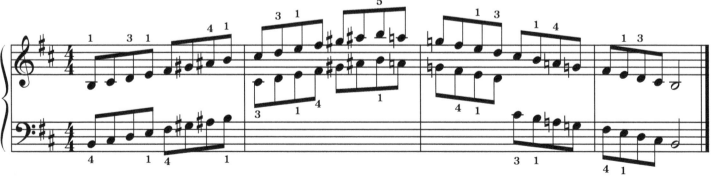

*In the 1st octave, LH 4 is used on B—LH 1 thereafter.

53

Key of F# Minor
Relative Minor of A Major

LH: 4th finger on F# (1st degree).   **RH:** 4th finger on G# (2nd degree).*

Natural minor scale, parallel motion in octaves.

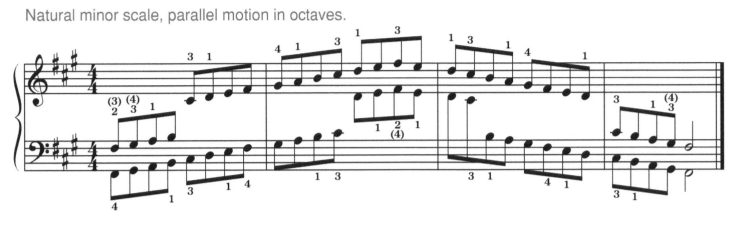

Harmonic minor scale, parallel motion in octaves.

Harmonic minor scale, contrary motion.

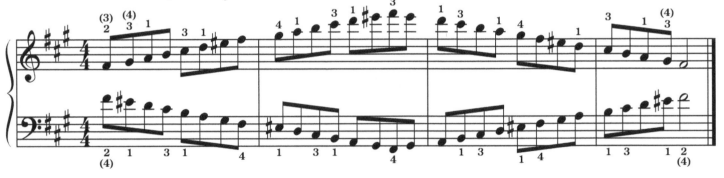

Melodic minor scale, parallel motion in octaves. RH 4th finger on D# ascending, G# descending.

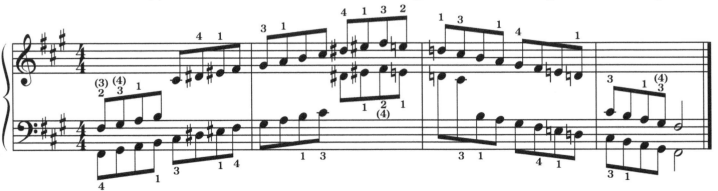

*In the 1st octave, RH 3 or 4 may be used on G#—RH 4 thereafter.

Key of C♯ Minor
Relative Minor of E Major

LH: 4th finger on F♯ (4th degree).   **RH:** 4th finger on D♯ (2nd degree).*

Natural minor scale, parallel motion in octaves.

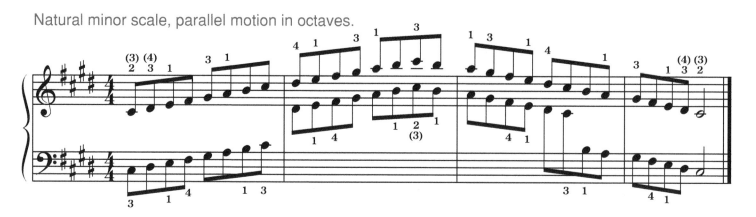

Harmonic minor scale, parallel motion in octaves.

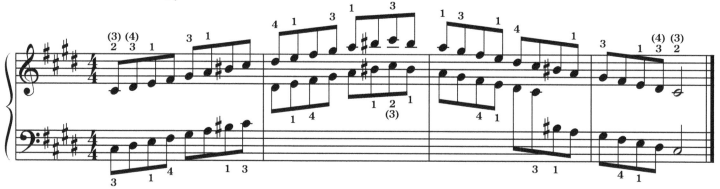

Harmonic minor scale, contrary motion.

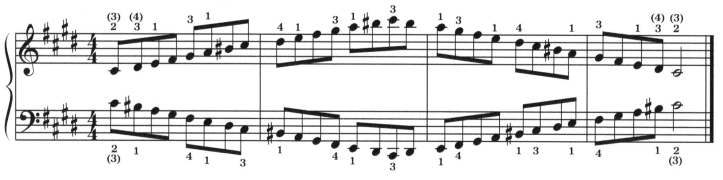

Melodic minor scale, parallel motion in octaves. RH 4th finger on A♯ ascending, D♯ descending.

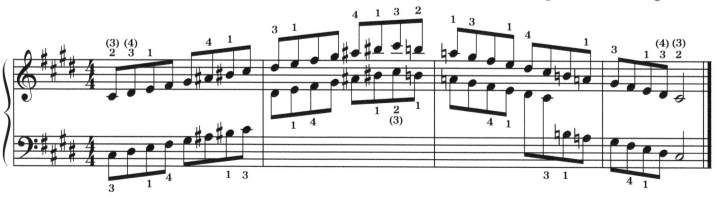

*In the 1st octave, RH 3 or 4 may be used on D♯—RH 4 thereafter.

C♯ Minor Triads Root position

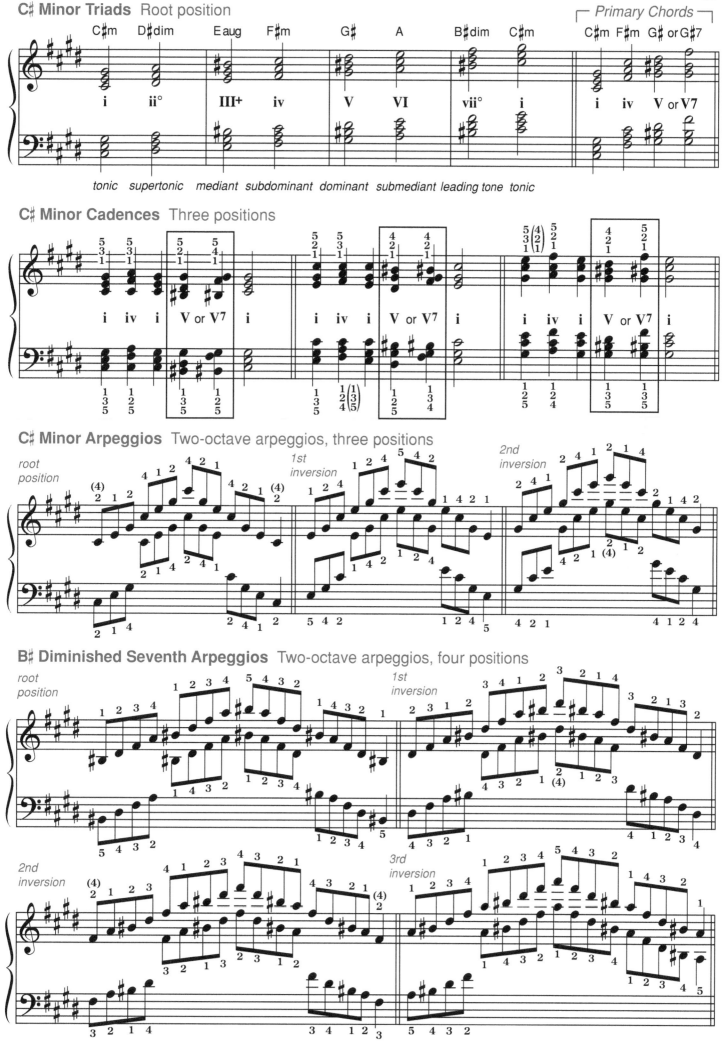

tonic   supertonic   mediant   subdominant   dominant   submediant   leading tone   tonic

C♯ Minor Cadences Three positions

C♯ Minor Arpeggios Two-octave arpeggios, three positions

B♯ Diminished Seventh Arpeggios Two-octave arpeggios, four positions

Key of G♯ Minor*
Relative Minor of B Major

LH: 4th finger on C♯ (4th degree). **RH:** 4th finger on A♯ (2nd degree).**

Natural minor scale, parallel motion in octaves. LH 4th finger on F♯ (7th degree).

This is the only scale where the LH fingering in the *natural* minor differs from the *harmonic* minor.

Harmonic minor scale, parallel motion in octaves.

Harmonic minor scale, contrary motion.

Melodic minor scale, parallel motion in octaves. LH 4th finger on C♯ ascending, F♯ descending.

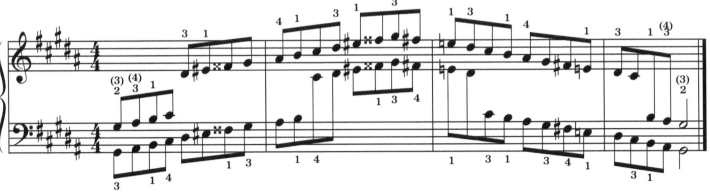

*Enharmonic with A♭ minor. See page 76.
**In the 1st octave, RH 3 or 4 may be used on A♯—RH 4 thereafter.

G♯ Minor Triads Root position

tonic supertonic mediant subdominant dominant submediant leading tone tonic

G♯ Minor Cadences Three positions

G♯ Minor Arpeggios Two-octave arpeggios, three positions

F✕ Diminished Seventh Arpeggios Two-octave arpeggios, four positions

Key of D♯ Minor*
Relative Minor of F♯ Major

LH: 4th finger on F♯ (3rd degree). **RH:** 4th finger on A♯ (5th degree).

Natural minor scale, parallel motion in octaves.

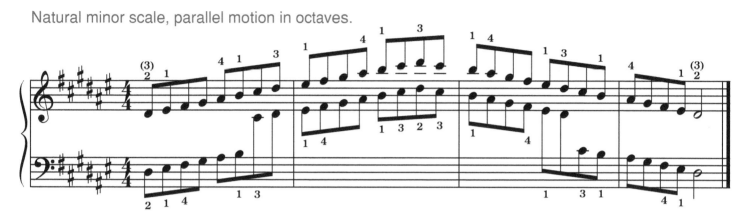

Harmonic minor scale, parallel motion in octaves.

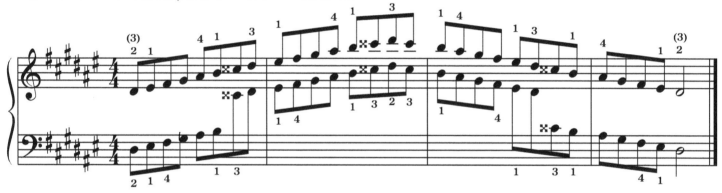

Harmonic minor scale, contrary motion.

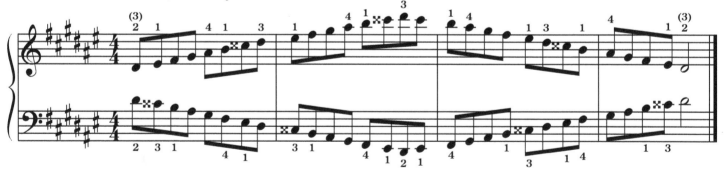

Melodic minor scale, parallel motion in octaves.

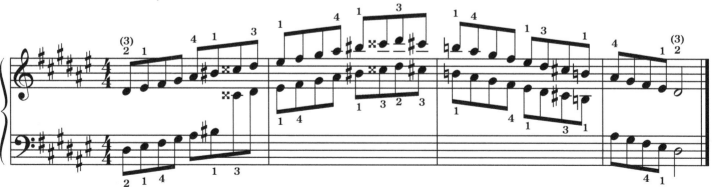

*Enharmonic with E♭ minor. See page 74.

Key of A♯ Minor*
Relative Minor of C♯ Major

LH: 4th finger on F♯ or F𝄪 (6th degree).   **RH:** 4th finger on A♯ (1st degree).**

Natural minor scale, parallel motion in octaves.

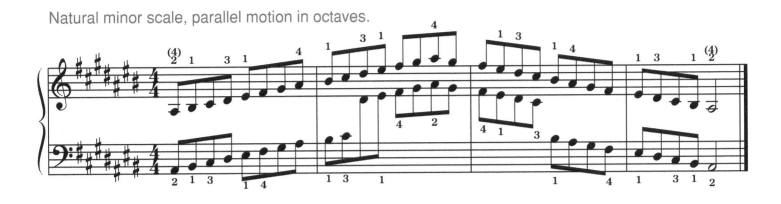

Harmonic minor scale, parallel motion in octaves.

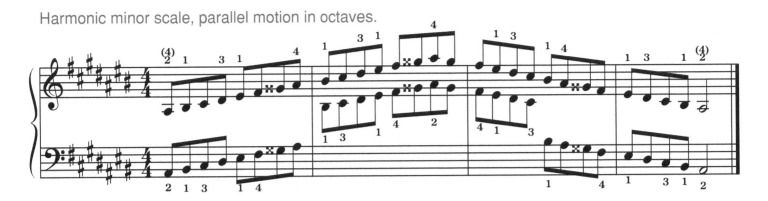

Harmonic minor scale, contrary motion.

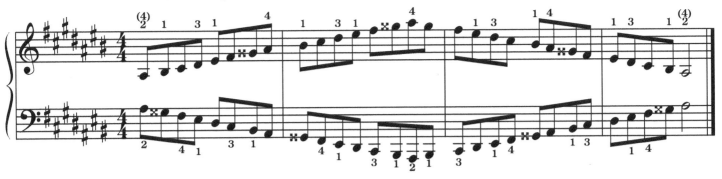

Melodic minor scale, parallel motion in octaves. LH 4 on F𝄪 ascending, F♯ descending.

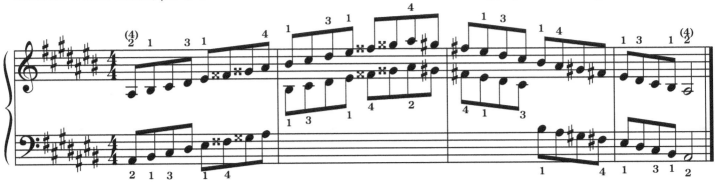

*Enharmonic with B♭ minor. See page 72.
**In the 1st octave, RH 2 or 4 may be used on the A♯—RH 4 thereafter.

Part 5

Key of D Minor
Relative Minor of F Major

LH: 4th finger on E (2nd degree of scale). **RH:** 4th finger on C or C♯ (7th degree of scale).*

Natural minor scale, parallel motion in octaves.

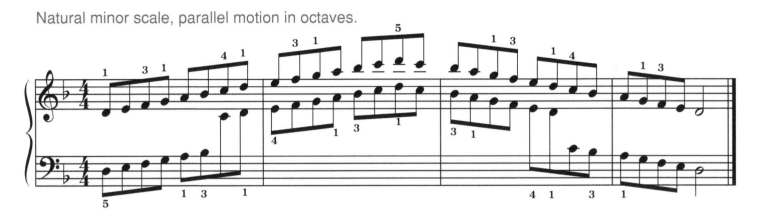

Harmonic minor scale, parallel motion in octaves.

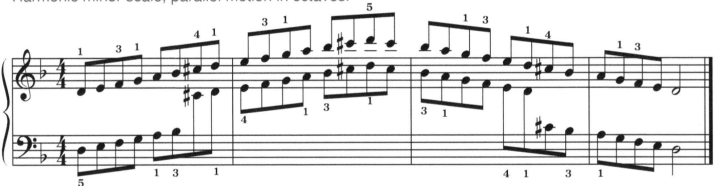

Harmonic minor scale, contrary motion.

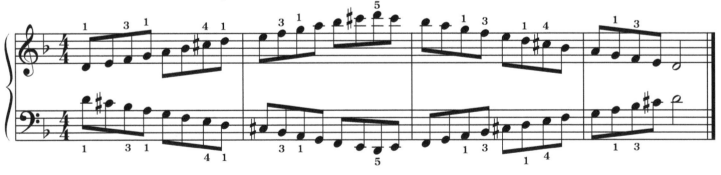

Melodic minor scale, parallel motion in octaves. RH 4th finger on C♯ ascending, C♮ descending.

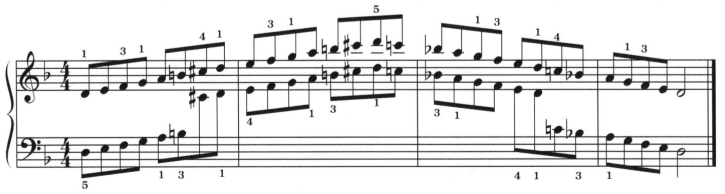

*For the importance of knowing the position of the 4th finger, see page 16, par. 4.

D Minor Triads Root position

tonic supertonic mediant subdominant dominant submediant leading tone tonic

D Minor Cadences Three positions

D Minor Arpeggios Two-octave arpeggios, three positions

C# Diminished Seventh Arpeggios Two-octave arpeggios, four positions

Key of G Minor
Relative Minor of B♭ Major

LH: 4th finger on A (2nd degree). **RH:** 4th finger on F or F♯ (7th degree).

Natural minor scale, parallel motion in octaves.

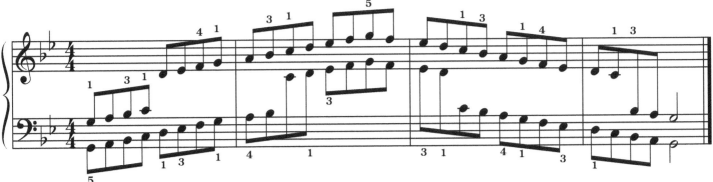

Harmonic minor scale, parallel motion in octaves.

Harmonic minor scale, contrary motion.

Melodic minor scale, parallel motion in octaves. RH 4th finger on F♯ ascending, F♮ descending.

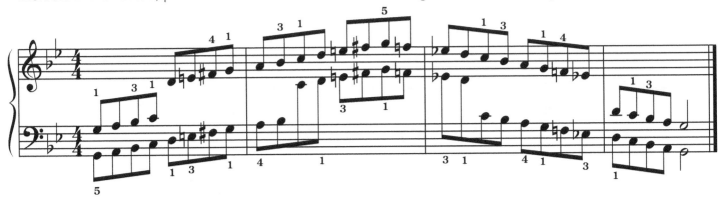

Key of C Minor
Relative Minor of E♭ Major

LH: 4th finger on D (2nd degree).   **RH:** 4th finger on B or B♭ (7th degree).

Natural minor scale, parallel motion in octaves.

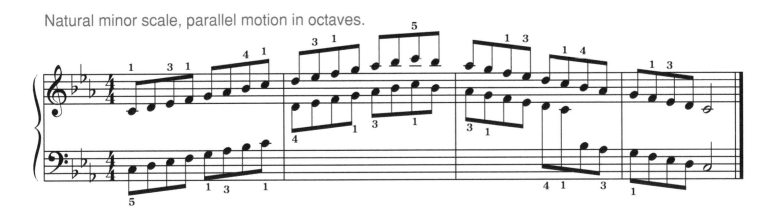

Harmonic minor scale, parallel motion in octaves.

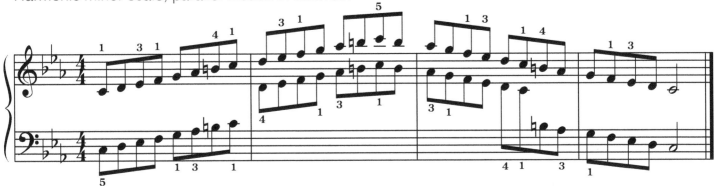

Harmonic minor scale, contrary motion.

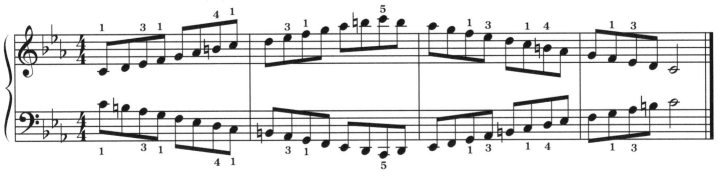

Melodic minor scale, parallel motion in octaves. RH 4th finger on B♮ ascending, B♭ descending.

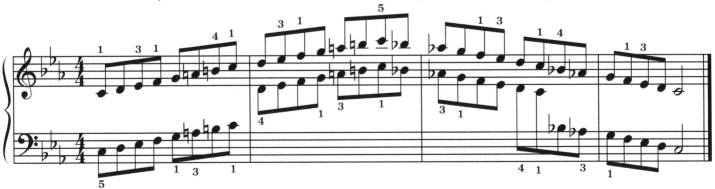

C Minor Triads Root position

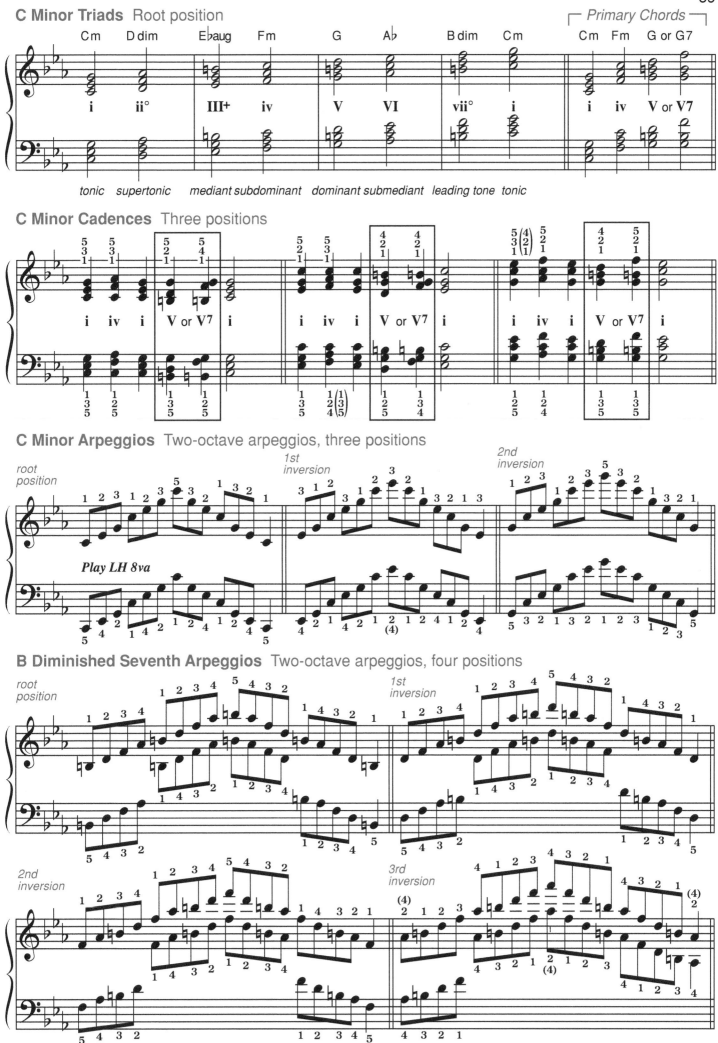

tonic   supertonic   mediant subdominant   dominant submediant   leading tone   tonic

C Minor Cadences Three positions

C Minor Arpeggios Two-octave arpeggios, three positions

B Diminished Seventh Arpeggios Two-octave arpeggios, four positions

Key of F Minor
Relative Minor of A♭ Major

LH: 4th finger on G (2nd degree).   **RH:** 4th finger on B♭ (4th degree).

Natural minor scale, parallel motion in octaves.

Harmonic minor scale, parallel motion in octaves.

Harmonic minor scale, contrary motion.

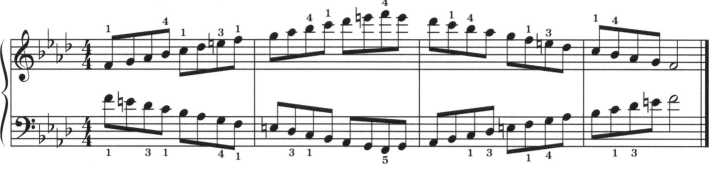

Melodic minor scale, parallel motion in octaves.

F Minor Triads Root position

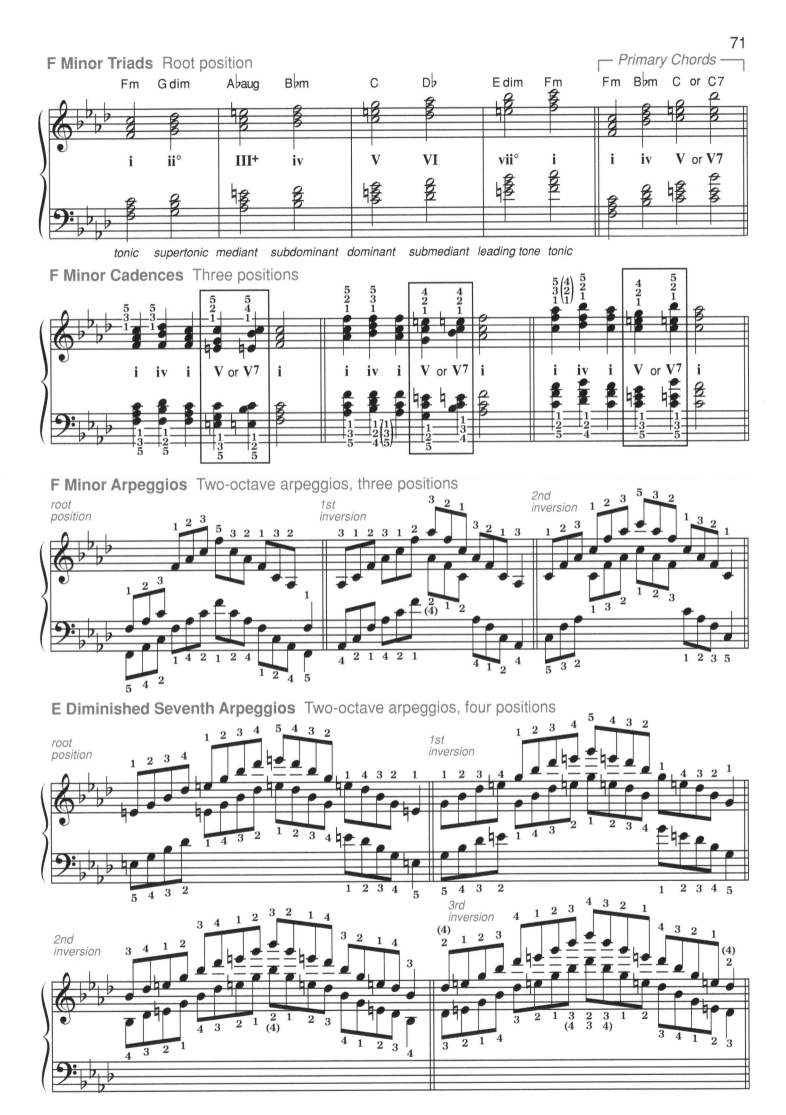

F Minor Cadences Three positions

F Minor Arpeggios Two-octave arpeggios, three positions

E Diminished Seventh Arpeggios Two-octave arpeggios, four positions

Key of B♭ Minor*
Relative Minor of D♭ Major

LH: 4th finger on G or G♭ (6th degree). **RH:** 4th finger on B♭ (1st degree).**

Natural minor scale, parallel motion in octaves.

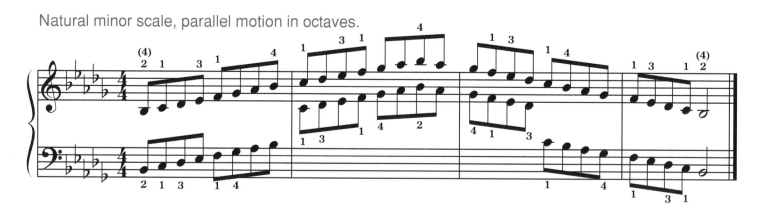

Harmonic minor scale, parallel motion in octaves.

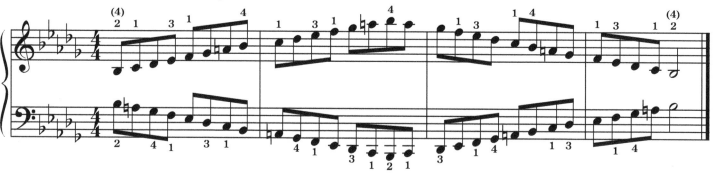

Harmonic minor scale, contrary motion.

Melodic minor scale, parallel motion in octaves. LH 4th finger on G♮ ascending, G♭ descending.

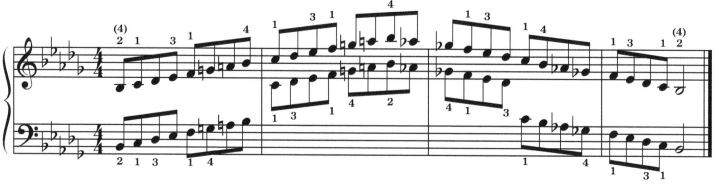

*Enharmonic with A♯ minor. See page 62.
**In the 1st octave, RH 2 or 4 may be used on B♭—RH 4 thereafter.

Key of E♭ Minor*

Relative Minor of G♭ Major

LH: 4th finger on G♭ (3rd degree).   **RH:** 4th finger on B♭ (5th degree).

Natural minor scale, parallel motion in octaves.

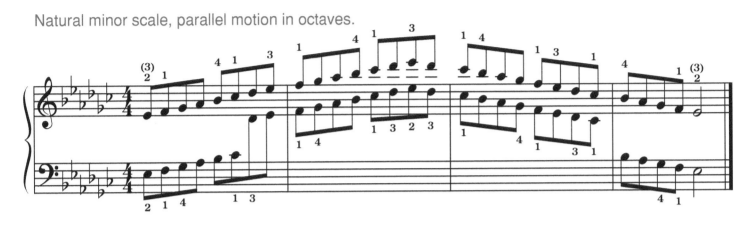

Harmonic minor scale, parallel motion in octaves.

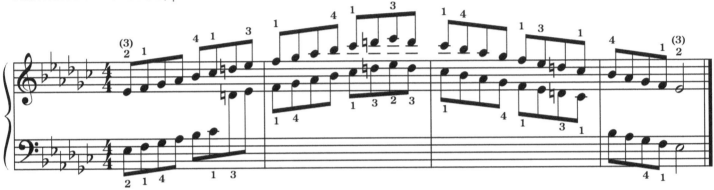

Harmonic minor scale, contrary motion.

Melodic minor scale, parallel motion in octaves.

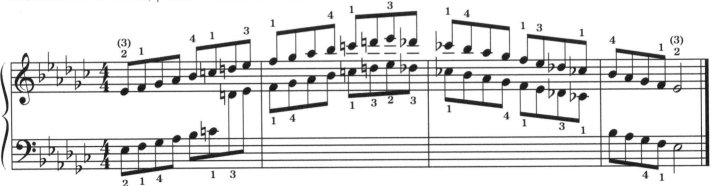

*Enharmonic with D♯ minor. See page 60.

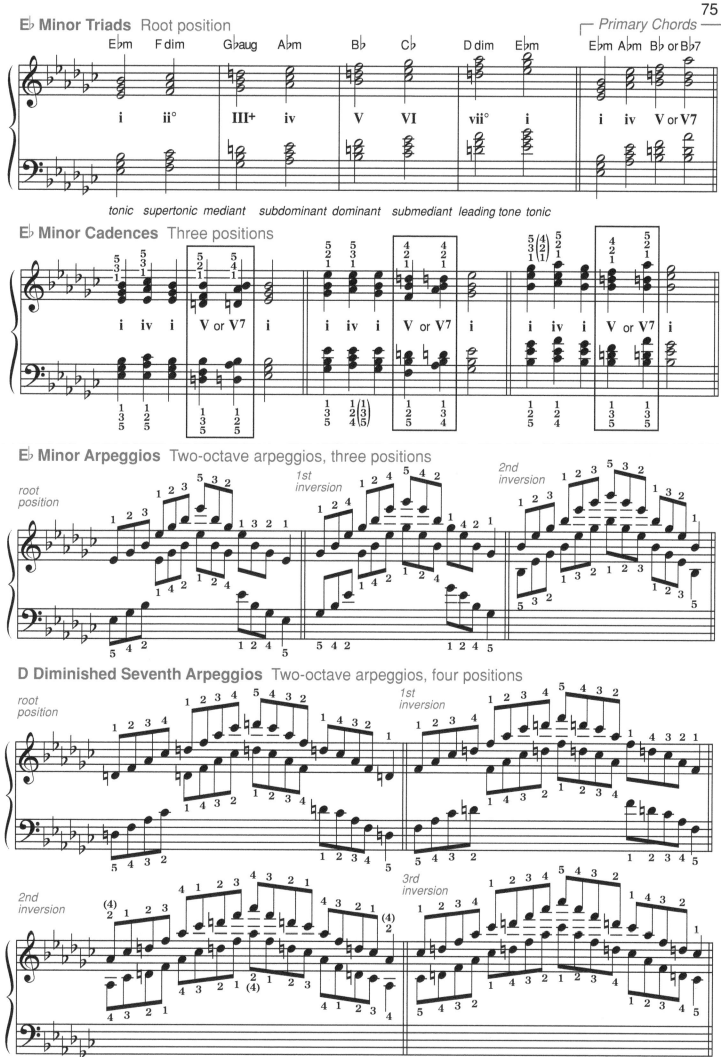

E♭ Minor Triads Root position

Primary Chords

E♭m   F dim   G♭aug   A♭m   B♭   C♭   D dim   E♭m   E♭m A♭m B♭ or B♭7

i   ii°   III+   iv   V   VI   vii°   i   i   iv   V or V7

tonic   supertonic   mediant   subdominant   dominant   submediant   leading tone   tonic

E♭ Minor Cadences Three positions

i   iv   i   V or V7   i   i   iv   i   V or V7   i   i   iv   i   V or V7   i

E♭ Minor Arpeggios Two-octave arpeggios, three positions

root position   1st inversion   2nd inversion

D Diminished Seventh Arpeggios Two-octave arpeggios, four positions

root position   1st inversion

2nd inversion   3rd inversion

Key of A♭ Minor*
Relative Minor of C♭ Major

LH: 4th finger on D♭ (4th degree).   **RH:** 4th finger on B♭ (2nd degree).**

Natural minor scale, parallel motion in octaves. LH 4th finger on G♭ (7th degree).

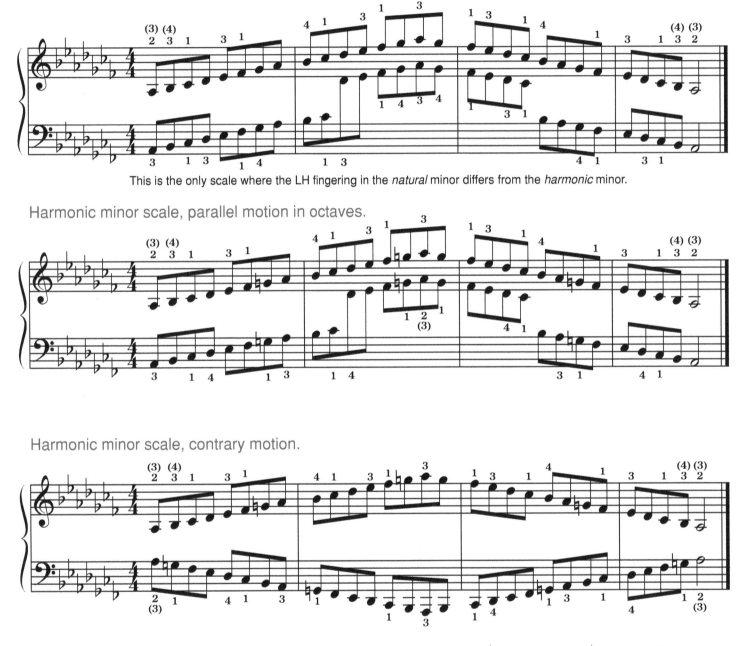

This is the only scale where the LH fingering in the *natural* minor differs from the *harmonic* minor.

Harmonic minor scale, parallel motion in octaves.

Harmonic minor scale, contrary motion.

Melodic minor scale, parallel motion in octaves. LH 4th finger on D♭ ascending, G♭ descending.

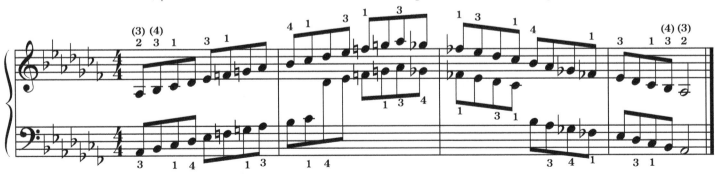

*Enharmonic with G♯ minor. See page 58.
**In the 1st octave, RH 3 or 4 may be used on B♭—RH 4 thereafter.

A♭ Minor Triads Root position

Primary Chords

A♭m B♭dim   C♭aug   D♭m   E♭   F♭aug   G dim   A♭m   A♭m   D♭m   E♭ or E♭7

i   ii°   III+   iv   V   VI   vii°   i   i   iv   V or V7

tonic supertonic mediant subdominant dominant submediant leading tone tonic

A♭ Minor Cadences Three positions

i   iv   i   V or V7   i   i   iv   i   V or V7   i   i   iv   i   V or V7   i

A♭ Minor Arpeggios Two-octave arpeggios, three positions

root position   *1st inversion*   *2nd inversion*

G Diminished Seventh Arpeggios Two-octave arpeggios, four positions

root position   *1st inversion*

2nd inversion   *3rd inversion*

78

Part 6

Chromatic Scales*
Parallel Motion

Parallel motion in octaves.

Parallel motion in minor thirds or tenths.

Parallel motion in major thirds or tenths.

Parallel motion in minor sixths.

Parallel motion in major sixths.

*For more information on chromatic scale fingering, see page 17.

Chromatic Scales
Contrary Motion

Contrary motion beginning in unison.

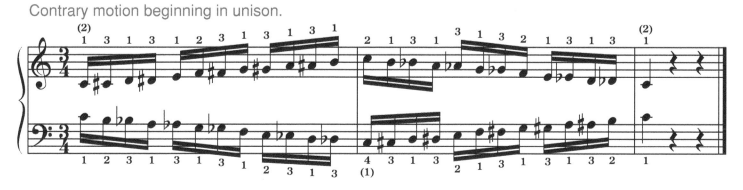

Contrary motion beginning at minor third or tenth.

Contrary motion at major third or tenth.

Contrary motion beginning at minor sixth.

Contrary motion beginning at major sixth.

Enrichment Options

The following enrichment options are designed to expand upon and extend the benefits of the technical exercises included in this book. They can be used with every key and are easy enough in concept so that they can be learned with little effort. The benefits of adding them, however, are invaluable in allowing the student to become proficient in all keys.

Harmonizing the Scales

Any of the following options may be used with the major and minor keys.

Chords in bass

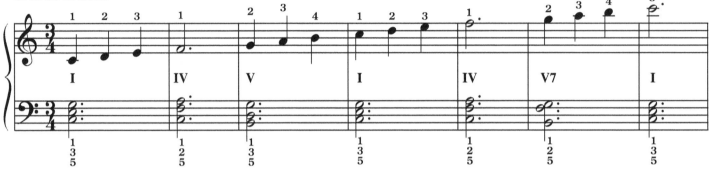

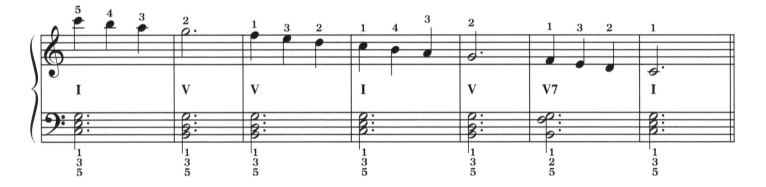

Chords in treble

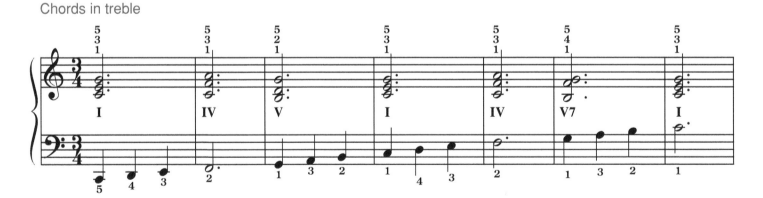

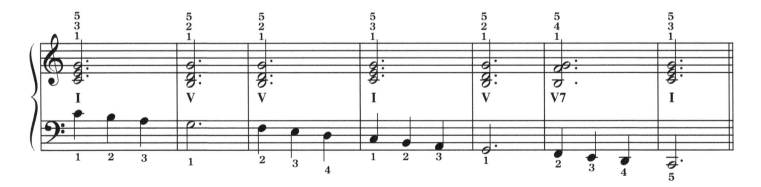

There are many well-known ways to play scales using various rhythms. Pianists also often create their own personal favorites. The following pages include scale patterns that are less well known and offer unique approaches to scale playing.

Blocked Scales

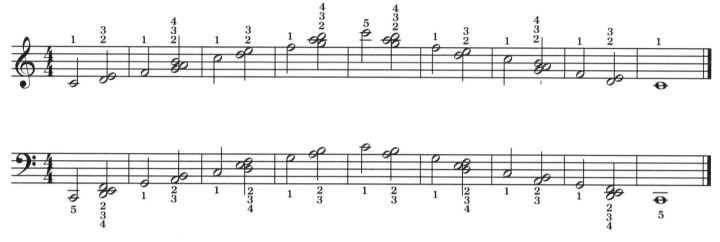

Accelerating Scales
Play LH one or two octaves lower than RH.

Expanding Scales No. 1

Play LH one or two octaves lower than RH.

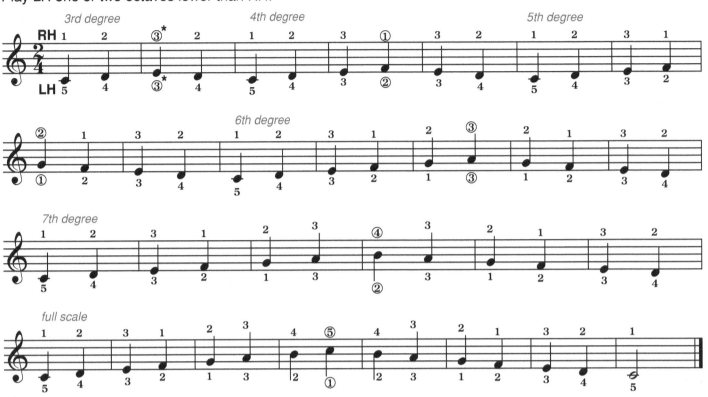

*Circled fingering represents the highest degree played in each expansion.

Expanding Scales No. 2

Begin with the finger that starts the second octave when playing two or more octaves.

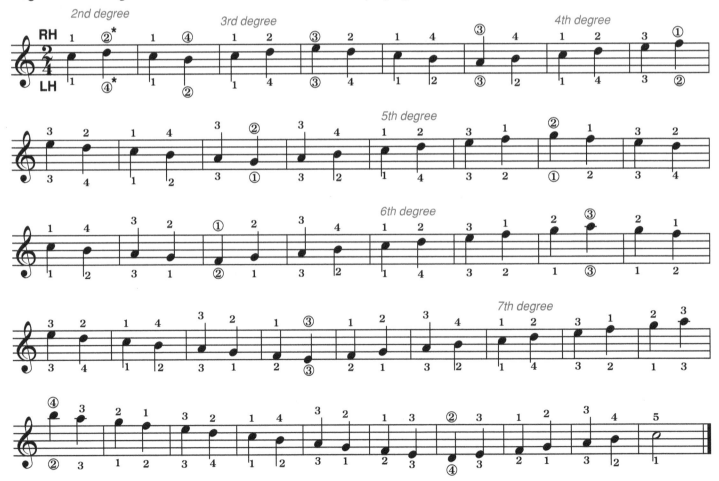

*Circled fingering represents the *highest* and *lowest* degree played in each expansion.

Scales in Double Thirds, Double Sixths and Octaves.

C major in double thirds—staccato only

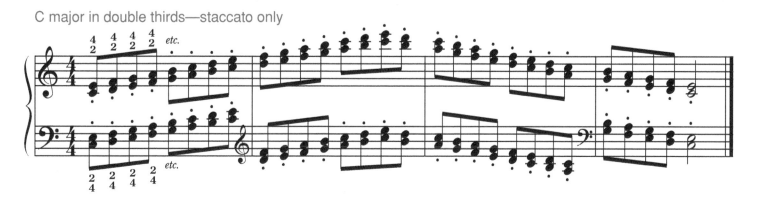

C major in double sixths—staccato only

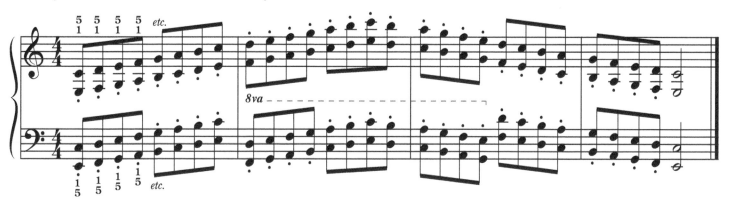

C major in octaves—staccato only (Optional: in scales using black keys, the thumb and 4th finger may be used on the black keys in both hands.)

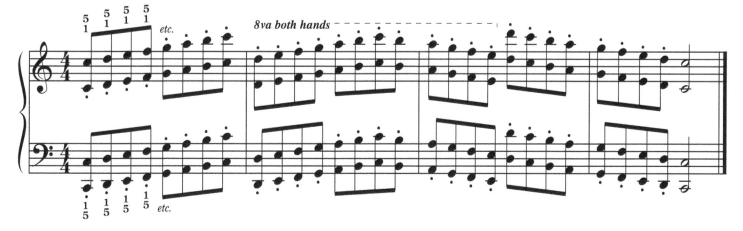

C major in double thirds—legato only.

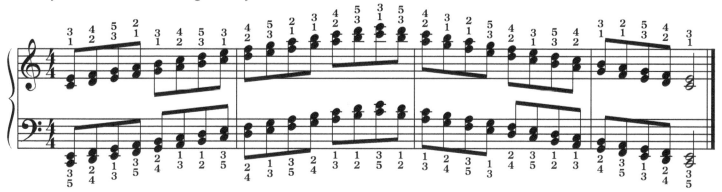

Scales—The Grand Form

The following SCALE ROUTINE is used by many piano conservatories and master piano teachers throughout the world. It may be used with all the major and minor scales.

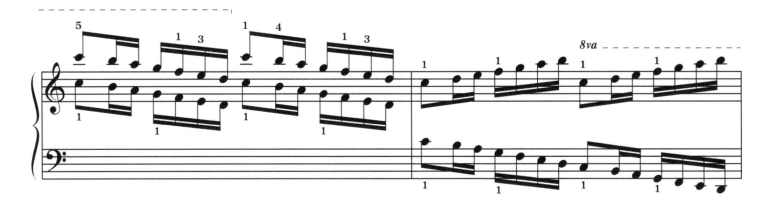

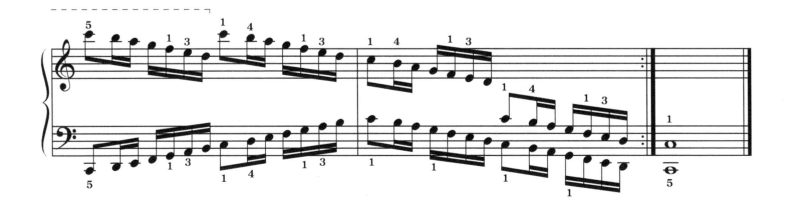

Broken Triads

Root position triads on every degree of the major scale.

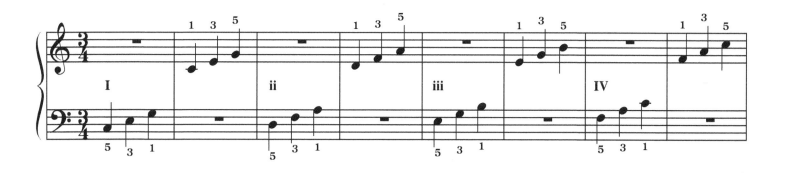

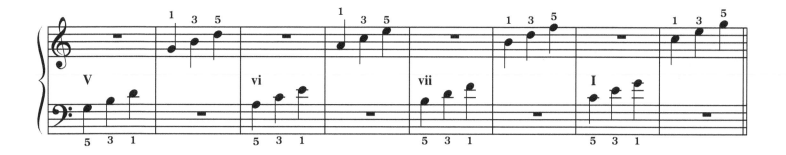

Root position triads on every degree of the harmonic minor scale.

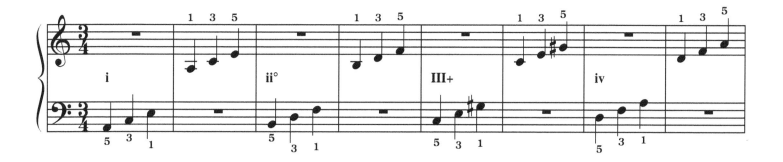

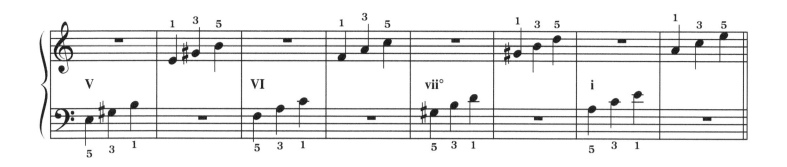

Triad Chain Broken and block

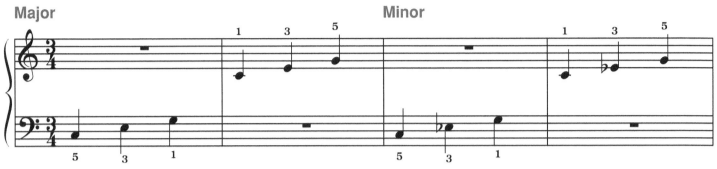

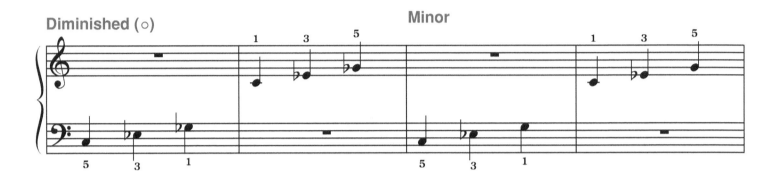

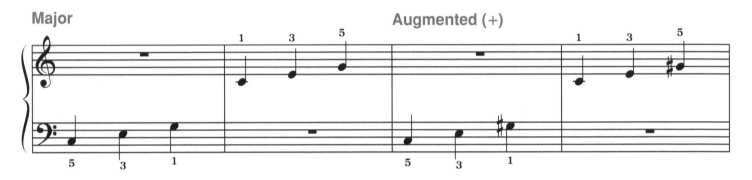

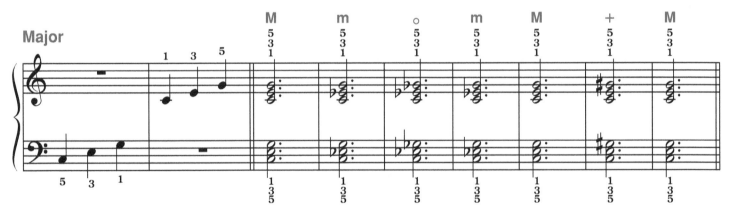

Cadences

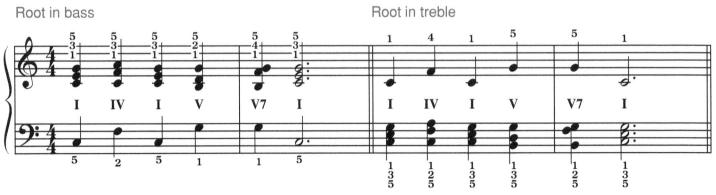

Triads Block and broken

Four-note form, block and broken

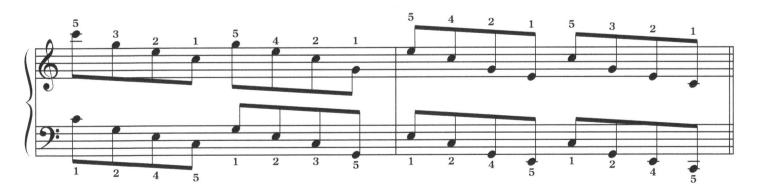

Four-note form, block and broken (alternate version)

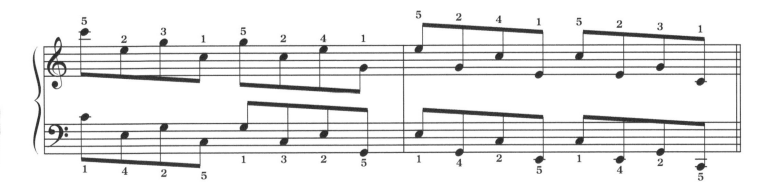

Major Scale Fingering Chart

Two octaves — ascending. Dot (•) over a finger number indicates to play a black key.

Key	Fingering
C	RH: 1 2 3 1 2 3 4 1 2 3 1 2 3 4 5
	LH: 5 4 3 2 1 3 2 1 4 3 2 1 3 2 1
G	RH: 1 2 3 1 2 3 4̇ 1 2 3 1 2 3 4̇ 5
	LH: 5 4 3 2 1 3 2 1 4 3 2 1 3 2 1
D	RH: 1 2 3̇ 1 2 3 4̇ 1 2 3̇ 1 2 3 4̇ 5
	LH: 5 4 3 2 1 3 2 1 4 3 2 1 3 2 1
A	RH: 1 2 3̇ 1 2 3̇ 4̇ 1 2 3̇ 1 2 3̇ 4̇ 5
	LH: 5 4 3 2 1 3 2 1 4 3 2 1 3 2 1
E	RH: 1 2̇ 3̇ 1 2 3 4̇ 1 2̇ 3̇ 1 2 3̇ 4̇ 5
	LH: 5 4 3 2 1 3 2 1 4 3 2 1 3 2 1
B	RH: 1 2̇ 3̇ 1 2̇ 3 4̇ 1 2̇ 3̇ 1 2̇ 3̇ 4 5
	LH: 4 3 2 1 4 3 2 1 3 2 1 4 3 2 1

Key	Fingering
G♭/ F♯	RH: 2̇ 3̇ 4̇ 1 2̇ 3̇ 1 2̇ 3̇ 4̇ 1 2̇ 3̇ 1 2̇
	LH: 4 3 2 1 3 2 1 4 3 2 1 3 2 1 2 (4)
D♭/ C♯	RH: 2̇ 3̇ 1 2̇ 3̇ 4̇ 1 2̇ 3̇ 1 2̇ 3̇ 4̇ 1 2̇
	LH: 3 2 1 4 3 2 1 3 2 1 4 3 2 1 2 (3)
A♭	RH: (3̇ 4̇) 2̇ 3̇ 1 2̇ 3̇ 1 2 3̇ 4̇ 1 2̇ 3̇ 1 2 3̇
	LH: 3 2 1 4 3 2 1 3 2 1 4 3 2 1 2 (3)
E♭	RH: (3̇) 2̇ 1 2 3̇ 4̇ 1 2 3̇ 1 2 3̇ 4̇ 1 2 3̇
	LH: 3 2 1 4 3 2 1 3 2 1 4 3 2 1 2 (3)
B♭	RH: (4̇) 2̇ 1 2 3̇ 1 2 3 4̇ 1 2 3̇ 1 2 3 4̇
	LH: 3 2 1 4 3 2 1 3 2 1 4 3 2 1 2 (3)
F	RH: 1 2 3 4̇ 1 2 3 1 2 3 4̇ 1 2 3 4̇
	LH: 5 4 3 2 1 3 2 1 4 3 2 1 3 2 1

Major Arpeggio Fingering Chart

Two octaves — ascending.

Key	Fingering
C	RH: 1 2 3 1 2 3 5
	LH: 5 4 2 1 4 2 1
G	RH: 1 2 3 1 2 3 5
	LH: 5 4 2 1 4 2 1
D	RH: 1 2̇ 3 1 2̇ 3 5
	LH: 5 3 2 1 3 2 1
A	RH: 1 2̇ 3 1 2̇ 3 5
	LH: 5 3 2 1 3 2 1
E	RH: 1 2̇ 3 1 2̇ 3 5
	LH: 5 3 2 1 3 2 1
B	RH: 1 2̇ 3̇ 1 2̇ 3̇ 5
	LH: 5 3 2 1 3 2 1

Key	Fingering
G♭/ F♯	RH: 1̇ 2̇ 3̇ 1̇ 2̇ 3̇ 5̇
	LH: 5 3 2 1 3 2 1
D♭/ C♯	RH: (4̇) 2̇ 1 2 4̇ 1 2̇ 4̇
	LH: 2 1 4 2 1 4 2 (3)
A♭	RH: (4̇) 2̇ 1 2 4̇ 1 2̇ 4̇
	LH: 2 1 4 2 1 4 2
E♭	RH: (4̇) 2̇ 1 2 4̇ 1 2̇ 4̇
	LH: 2 1 4 2 1 4 2
B♭	RH: (4̇) 2̇ 1 2 4̇ 1 2̇ 4̇
	LH: 3 2 1 3 2 1 2 (3)
F	RH: 1 2 3 1 2 3 5
	LH: 5 4 2 1 4 2 1